The Stay-at-Home Moms' Year-Round Outfit Guide: 280+ *Outfits for the Entire Year*

By: Corina Holden
www.nowthaticando.com
www.frumpfighters.com

The Stay-at-Home Moms' Year-Round Outfit Guide: 280+ Outfits for the Entire Year

By Corina Holden

Frumpy Fighters LLC

www.frumpfighters.com and www.nowthaticando.com

nowthaticando@gmail.com

Copyright © 2016-2019 Frumpy Fighters LLC

All rights reserved. This ebook is intended for personal use only. Printing for personal use is permitted. Sending the ebook to others or printing additional copies to give to others is not permitted. They will need to obtain their own copy, or a copy can be gifted (see below).

An additional copy may be purchased for gifting to a friend at www.frumpfighters.com/outfit-guides-checkout. Choose "Gift Order" and use code FRIENDSHIP at checkout for 20% off your gift order.

Table of Contents

	Page
About This Guide	6
PART 1: Step-by-Step Instructions for Using This Guide	8
Steps to Updating Your Wardrobe	10
PART 2: The Capsule Plan Visuals & Checklist	12
The Capsule Plan Visuals	13
The Capsule Plan Checklist	27
PART 3: The Outfits*	33
The Outfit Gallery Web App	34
How to View the Outfits On Real People	35
How to Read the Outfit Pages	36
Outfits 1-51: Casual Outfits for Fall	38
Outfits 52-61: Dressy Outfits for Fall	70
Outfits 62-105: Casual Outfits for Winter	76
Outfits 106-115: Dressy Outfits for Winter	105
Outfits 116-168: Casual Outfits for Spring	112
Outfits 169-178: Dressy Outfits for Spring	146
Outfits 179-229: Casual Outfits for Summer	153
Outfits 230-239: Dressy Outfits for Summer	185
PART 4: The Appendix	192
Bonus Resources Included With Outfit Guide	193
Dashboard Access	194
Shop Related Resources	195

* Outfits that are new to this outfit guide are marked with an "a" rather than a new number (e.g. Outfit #3a). Look for the 44 new outfits intermixed among the 239 other outfits. This brings the total number of outfits in this guide to 288. To view just the new outfits together, use the outfit gallery web app or the "New Outfits" booklet (access both from your dashboard).

About This Guide

Hey Mama!

Thanks for purchasing the *Stay-at-Home Moms' Year-Round Outfit Guide!*

My name is Corina and I'm thrilled that you've joined us! I'm a mom of three boys and create these outfit guides to help myself and other moms dress cute and classy without compromising the need for comfort and a budget.

I started blogging about mom fashion after I became a stay-at-home mommy and realized how easy it was to look "frumpy" every day.

I was tired and had less time to get dressed in the morning, go shopping, or even keep up with fashion.

Through my blogging, I was fascinated to learn how simple it could be to have a cute and up-to-date wardrobe without breaking the bank. *There is so much more than yoga pants and a tee out there that is just as comfy!*

It all comes down to having a plan
When you're deliberate about what goes in your wardrobe, you can explode your options for cute mom outfits right out of your closet! Get ready to join our ranks and feel like an incredibly cute and stylish mommy... perhaps for the first time in your life! That was certainly the case for me.

How this guide works
Having a plan for your wardrobe sounds like a great idea until you're faced with the need to come up with one. I know the feeling of overwhelm as you try to figure out what you should even have in your wardrobe. How do you know what pieces are still in style or which pieces mix and match with each other?

This outfit guide does all the work for you by providing you with a wardrobe plan specially designed for moms. All the pieces are carefully planned to cover all your wardrobe needs while helping you look on trend and create tons of outfit options.

In Parts 1 & 2 of this guide, I'll walk you through how to apply the wardrobe plan to what you already own. You'll have the freedom to fill in the gaps in your wardrobe as time and budget allows.

Then in Part 3 I'll show you all of the ways the pieces combine into mom-friendly outfits. Not only will you finally maximize the use of everything in your wardrobe, but you'll learn how to properly style different kinds of outfits. Believe it or not, in no time you will get good at creating your own Pinterest-worthy looks!

Not sure about a *capsule* wardrobe?
Don't worry, we're all about flexibility here. While traditional capsule wardrobes are very limited in size, I simply use the capsule concept to provide an easy-to-follow framework for your wardrobe. You can add more pieces within each suggested category to make your wardrobe whatever size you want. You can also swap out to your heart's content... just make it yours!

How this guide is laid out
- ***Part 1: Step-by-Step Instructions for Updating Your Wardrobe.*** How to update your wardrobe starting with what you already own.
- ***Part 2: The Capsule Plan.*** Visuals of example pieces so that you capture the vision of the overall wardrobe plan & printable checklist that you can use to shop your closet and add some fresh new items to your wardrobe as the budget allows.
- ***Part 3: The Outfits.*** The 288 ways the pieces in the capsule plan combine into mom-friendly outfits!
- ***Part 4: The Appendix/Bonus Resources.*** How to access the bonus resources that come with your outfit guide.

Let's get started!

All my best,
Corina

www.frumpfighters.com or
www.nowthaticando.com

Part 1

Step-By-Step Instructions for Updating Your Wardrobe

Ok, so you've got clothes in your closet. Don't we all! BUT if you're like the rest of us mamas, you feel like your wardrobe doesn't match up with your current life needs or it's just so badly in need of updating that you just resort to the easy jeans and tee every day.

This is normal! Having babies changes so much (especially our bodies) and it's often our last priority to take the time to keep up with our wardrobes.

Starting on the next page I'll show you the simple steps you can follow to REFRESH your wardrobe. And you don't need an ounce of fashion experience because I do all the research for us to suggest a set of mom-friendly wardrobe pieces that look on point without feeling too trendy.

The Key: The key to a simplified wardrobe is making sure all the pieces are "remixable" (easy to mix and match). This allows you to have fewer pieces and yet create more variety in your daily looks.

To make a wardrobe "remixable," you need these characteristics:
1. A set color palette/color scheme that you (mostly) stick to
2. A variety of pieces (going beyond jeans and tees!)
3. A proper ratio of pieces in neutral colors versus complementary colors and solid fabrics versus pattern fabrics

While you could certainly set out to configure this for yourself, it can take a lot of expensive trial and error to achieve the perfect balance.

That's why this guide does that for you, providing you with a complete wardrobe plan framework that takes all of this into account. All you have to do is apply the plan to YOU.

The next page will lay those steps out easily.

Steps to Updating Your Wardrobe

Set aside a little time for yourself. This can be an entire evening to yourself, or just an hour or two during your kids' nap time. Grab a snack and your favorite beverage. Give yourself grace and plan to have fun!

If you're feeling frustrated or alone, join the party in our supportive Facebook group: www.nowthaticando.com/facebook-group
(See? You're not alone! You've got this!)

> **I've Got Your Back** For additional support with these steps, complete them within the "Customize Your Capsule" mini course that comes with your outfit guide. Access the mini course from your dashboard. Instructions in the [Appendix](#).

STEP 1 **Clean Out The Clutter.** Go through all your clothes (hanging, folded, in hamper-jail) and place *just your favorite pieces* on the bed. These are pieces that fit you well, are in good condition, and you find yourself going back to over and over.

For everything left hanging or folded (didn't make your "favorites" cut), place each item in one of three piles:
1. Too old -> Toss
2. Never worn/doesn't fit/don't like -> Donate or Consign
3. Might use in the future/unsure -> Archive by storing in a bin or a spare closet. Set a reminder on your phone to reassess these items in 3 months.

Place your favorite pieces back in your closet/drawers.

STEP 2 **Print The Capsule.** If you haven't already, go ahead and print out this guide. To save on ink, print just the capsule plan checklist.

STEP 3 **Customize the Plan To Your Needs and Preferences.**
- *Customize Colors.* Look over the Capsule Plan Visuals page. See the suggested color palette? This is just an example of how you can plan a set of colors to stick with as you move forward. You can swap your own colors in to make it your own! (Use the blank color template on the checklist page.)

STEP 3 (cont.)
- *Customize Pieces.* Take a look at the suggested pieces on the visuals page. If you find that something wouldn't work for your style or body shape, swap it out for something similar that you prefer! Scribble and make notes about anything you want to swap.

STEP 4 **Capsule Check Off.** Now take the visuals and checklist and go through your freshly de-cluttered closet. Check off items you have. *You do not need to have the exact pieces.* Follow the criteria I've used within the label of each piece. For example: "Neutral Tunic Top" means it should be a tunic length top in a solid neutral color from the color palette you planned. Beyond these specifications, your pieces can vary from the example pieces and still achieve remixability.

STEP 5 **Shop For What's Left.** Anything left unchecked on your checklist becomes your shopping list! Easy, right? To make shopping go quickly, take a moment to specify what colors you're aiming to find for each item. This makes it easier to browse the images online and racks in-store.

Shopping Tips It's hard to get out shopping with kids in tow! I do most of my shopping online. You can click the exact item labels on the visuals page to purchase it online. For additional shopping links, use the Shopping Guide included with this book (access via dashboard; see Appendix).
You can also do your own browsing online. The following are tried and true favorites used by our community of moms:
- Amazon.com - Prime offers free shipping and free returns. Prime Wardrobe also allows you to try on items for 7 days free.
- Jane.com* - This website offers affordable, limited-time deals on gorgeous women's apparel. You'll find most of the recommended items from this capsule for sale here! (Sign up for their email list to get notified when a deal goes live--the best items sell out fast.)
- Target.com*, HM.com/en_us*, OldNavy.com* - All these popular retailers offer free returns (Old Navy pays return shipping. Target and H&M offer free returns in-store).

---

*Affiliate links. I earn a small commission on purchases made through these links at no cost to you!

Part 2

The Capsule Plan
Visuals & Checklist

The Capsule Plan Visuals

Now we get to the fun part! The next few pages show you which pieces I recommend for a well-rounded and stylish, but comfy, mom wardrobe.

Not into small capsule wardrobes? This capsule plan is just the framework I use to lay out the wardrobe essentials. It can be adapted to any size by simply adding pieces within any of the categories.

Does it seem big? Remember this covers all seasons of the year! You most likely already have many of the pieces in your closet. For pieces you don't own yet, just take your time adding them as the budget allows.

This capsule plan is carefully crafted to allow tons of outfit variety. You can create over 280 unique outfits with just the tops/bottoms and dresses! That's not counting all the variations you can create with the completer pieces and accessories.

When using this list to get your wardrobe together, focus on the label and additional notes provided for each piece. Your pieces don't have to look exactly the same; they just need the same characteristics listed in the label and notes in order to create the same number of outfits.

Want to pin this to your clothing board on Pinterest? Visit the following blog post for the pin in full resolution:

https://nowthaticando.com/home/full-year-wardrobe-capsule-plan-for-moms

KEY

This capsule plan uses the following example color palette to demonstrate how you would apply your color scheme to the pieces. Swap in your own colors using the blank template on the checklist page to customize it to your taste.

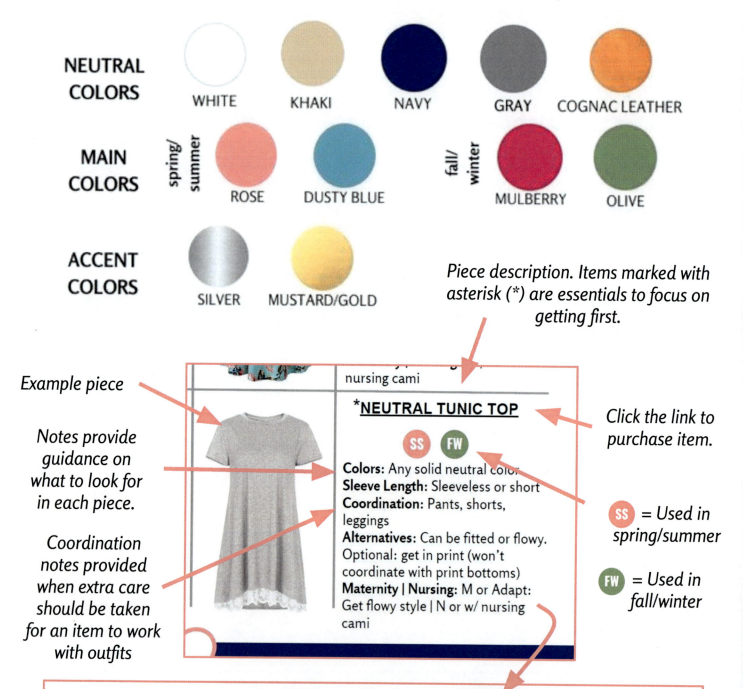

NEUTRAL COLORS: WHITE, KHAKI, NAVY, GRAY, COGNAC LEATHER

MAIN COLORS:
- spring/summer: ROSE, DUSTY BLUE
- fall/winter: MULBERRY, OLIVE

ACCENT COLORS: SILVER, MUSTARD/GOLD

Example piece

Notes provide guidance on what to look for in each piece.

Coordination notes provided when extra care should be taken for an item to work with outfits

Piece description. Items marked with asterisk (*) are essentials to focus on getting first.

Click the link to purchase item.

*NEUTRAL TUNIC TOP

SS FW

Colors: Any solid neutral color
Sleeve Length: Sleeveless or short
Coordination: Pants, shorts, leggings
Alternatives: Can be fitted or flowy. Optional: get in print (won't coordinate with print bottoms)
Maternity | Nursing: M or Adapt: Get flowy style | N or w/ nursing cami

SS = *Used in spring/summer*

FW = *Used in fall/winter*

Key for Maternity/Nursing Notes

M = Get maternity version of this piece
Adapt = Use recommended tips to adapt a regular piece for maternity
N = Get nursing friendly style such a nursing design, wrap style, henley, or button-down
W/ nursing cami = Use a regular top with a nursing cami underneath

TOPS

*CHAMBRAY BUTTON-DOWN

Colors: Light or Dark Denim
Sleeve Length: Long
Coordination: -
Alternatives: Pullover style
Maternity | Nursing: M or Adapt: Wear open, partially open, closed and knotted above belly, or belted over tee or tank

*SHORT SLEEVE STRIPED TEE

Colors: Classic stripes (white on navy/black, navy/black on white)
Sleeve Length: Sleeveless or short
Coordination: Floral scarf, Kimono
Alternatives: -
Maternity | Nursing: M | N or w/ nursing cami

LONG SLEEVE STRIPED TEE

Colors: Classic stripes (white on navy/black, navy/black on white)
Sleeve Length: Long
Coordination: Floral scarf
Alternatives: -
Maternity | Nursing: M | N or w/ nursing cami

*WHITE BASIC TEE

Colors: White
Sleeve Length: Short
Coordination: -
Alternatives: -
Maternity | Nursing: M | N or w/ nursing cami

WHITE FASHION TEE

Colors: White
Sleeve Length: Short
Coordination: -
Alternatives: Peplum, twist tee, button down
Maternity | Nursing: M | N or w/ nursing cami

*GRAY TEE

Colors: Gray, charcoal
Sleeve Length: Short sleeve
Coordination: -
Alternatives: -
Maternity | Nursing: M | N or w/ nursing cami

*LONG SLEEVE NAVY TEE

Colors: Dark neutral
Sleeve Length: Long
Coordination: -
Alternatives: Short sleeve for hot climates
Maternity | Nursing: M | N or w/ nursing cami

COLOR TEE

Colors: Main spring/summer color
Sleeve Length: Short
Coordination: Print bottoms
Alternatives: -
Maternity | Nursing: M | N or w/ nursing cami

TOPS

*PRINT TEE #1

Colors: Any print in main spring/summer or neutral colors
Sleeve Length: Short
Coordination: Color shorts & pants
Alternatives: Any print
Maternity | Nursing: M | N or w/ nursing cami

PRINT TEE #2

Colors: Any print in main spring/summer or neutral colors
Sleeve Length: Short
Coordination: Color shorts & pants
Alternatives: Any print
Maternity | Nursing: M | N or w/ nursing cami

*COLOR SLEEVELESS TOP #1

Colors: Main spring/summer color
Sleeve Length: Sleeveless
Coordination: -
Alternatives: Short sleeve
Maternity | Nursing: M | N or w/ nursing cami

COLOR SLEEVELESS TOP #2

Colors: Main spring/summer color
Sleeve Length: Sleeveless
Coordination: -
Alternatives: Short sleeve
Maternity | Nursing: M | N or w/ nursing cami

PRINT SLEEVELESS TOP #1

Colors: Any print in main spring/summer or neutral colors
Sleeve Length: Sleeveless or short
Coordination: Color shorts & pants. Button-down optional.
Alternatives: Short sleeve
Maternity | Nursing: M | N or w/ nursing cami

PRINT SLEEVELESS TOP #2

Colors: Any print in main spring/summer or neutral colors
Sleeve Length: Sleeveless or short
Coordination: Color shorts & pants.
Alternatives: Short sleeve
Maternity | Nursing: M | N or w/ nursing cami

*NEUTRAL FITTED TANK

Colors: Any solid neutral color
Sleeve Length: Sleeveless
Coordination: Used for layering
Alternatives: -
Maternity | Nursing: M | N or w/ nursing cami

*NEUTRAL TUNIC TOP

Colors: Any solid neutral color
Sleeve Length: Sleeveless or short
Coordination: Pants, shorts, leggings
Alternatives: Can be fitted or flowy. Optional: get in print (won't coordinate with print bottoms)
Maternity | Nursing: M or Adapt: Get flowy style | N or w/ nursing cami

Copyright © 2016-2019 Frumpy Fighters LLC   WWW.NOWTHATICANDO.COM

TOPS

GRAPHIC TEE

Colors: Any solid neutral, main or accent color + graphic
Sleeve Length: Sleeveless or short
Coordination: Color bottoms
Alternatives: Slogan or solid tee
Maternity | Nursing: M | N or w/ nursing cami

SLOGAN TEE

Colors: Any solid neutral, main or accent color + slogan
Sleeve Length: Short
Coordination: Color bottoms
Alternatives: Graphic or solid tee
Maternity | Nursing: M | N or w/ nursing cami

COLOR DRESSY TOP

Colors: Any main or accent color
Sleeve Length: Sleeveless, short, or quarter
Coordination: Print bottoms
Alternatives: Any dressy style
Maternity | Nursing: M | N or w/ nursing cami

*NEUTRAL DRESSY TOP

Colors: Any neutral
Sleeve Length: Sleeveless, short, or quarter
Coordination: -
Alternatives: Any dressy style
Maternity | Nursing: M | N or w/ nursing cami

PRINT DRESSY TOP

Colors: Any print in neutral, main or accent colors
Sleeve Length: Sleeveless, short, or quarter
Coordination: Color bottoms
Alternatives: Any dressy style
Maternity | Nursing: M | N or w/ nursing cami

*NEUTRAL PLAID BUTTON-DOWN

Colors: Any neutral-color plaid
Sleeve Length: Long
Coordination: -
Alternatives: Solid neutral button-down
Maternity | Nursing: M or Adapt: Wear open, partially open, closed and knotted above belly, or belted over tee or tank

COLOR PLAID BUTTON-DOWN

Colors: Any main or accent colors
Sleeve Length: Long
Coordination: Olive pants
Alternatives: Solid neutral button-down
Maternity | Nursing: M or Adapt: Wear open, partially open, closed and knotted above belly, or belted over tee or tank

*COLOR FITTED SWEATER

Colors: Any main or accent color
Sleeve Length: Long
Coordination: Print skirt
Alternatives: Crew neck, turtleneck
Maternity | Nursing: M | N or w/ nursing cami

Copyright © 2016-2019 Frumpy Fighters LLC   WWW.NOWTHATICANDO.COM

TOPS

NEUTRAL SLOUCHY SWEATER
 FW

Colors: Any neutral color
Sleeve Length: Long
Coordination: -
Alternatives: Short or tunic style
Maternity | Nursing: M or Adapt: Regular in longer style should work for most of pregnancy | N or w/ nursing cami

*NEUTRAL TUNIC SWEATER
 FW

Colors: Any neutral color
Sleeve Length: Long
Coordination: -
Alternatives: V-neck, crew neck
Maternity | Nursing: M or Adapt: Regular should work for most of pregnancy | N or w/ nursing cami

DRESSES

PRINT KNEE-LENGTH DRESS
 SS FW

Colors: Any print in neutral, main, or accent colors
Sleeve Length: Sleeveless, short
Coordination: Color tee & flats
Alternatives: Any simple, casual style. Midi, maxi length.
Maternity | Nursing: M | N (exact dress is maternity & nursing-friendly)

CHAMBRAY DRESS
 SS FW

Colors: Light or dark denim
Sleeve Length: Sleeveless, short
Coordination: -
Alternatives: Also called "denim dress"
Maternity | Nursing: M | N (exact dress is maternity & nursing-friendly)

*NEUTRAL KNEE-LENGTH DRESS
 SS FW

Colors: Any neutral color
Sleeve Length: Sleeveless, short
Coordination: -
Alternatives: Any simple, casual style, midi or maxi length
Maternity | Nursing: M | N

*STRIPED DRESS
 SS FW

Colors: Classic stripes (white on navy/black, navy/black on white)
Sleeve Length: Short, sleeveless, or quarter
Coordination: Kimono
Alternatives: Any simple, casual style, midi or maxi length
Maternity | Nursing: M | N

*BLACK MAXI DRESS
 SS FW

Colors: Black, taupe, charcoal, navy
Sleeve Length: Sleeveless, short
Coordination: -
Alternatives: Simple, jersey black dress in any style
Maternity | Nursing: M | N. Regular empire waist in stretchy material may work for pregnancy.

BOTTOMS

*DARK WASH JEANS

Colors: Dark wash blue denim
Fit: Skinny or slim fit (to wear with riding boots)
Coordination: -
Alternatives: Can get second pair in straight or bootcut if desired

LIGHT WASH JEANS

Colors: Medium or light wash blue denim
Fit: Slim or straight fit (need to be able to cuff easily)
Coordination: -
Alternatives: Boyfriend/girlfriend jeans. Distressing for trendier look.

*NEUTRAL JEANS

Colors: White, black, navy, gray, rust, or khaki
Fit: Skinny or slim fit (to wear with riding boots)
Coordination: -
Alternatives: Chino/twill material. Straight or bootcut.

*OLIVE PANTS

Colors: Any shade olive
Fit: Skinny or slim fit (to wear with riding boots)
Coordination: Shade of olive should work with your main colors, esp. for fall/winter.
Alternatives: Burgundy pants (limited to use in fall/winter). Straight or bootcut fit.

COLOR PANTS

Colors: Any main or accent color. Recommended to get color that works in all seasons.
Fit: Skinny, slim, or straight
Coordination: Print tops & scarves
Alternatives: Color denim. Bootcut.

SLIM FIT ATHLETIC PANTS

Colors: Black, navy, or gray
Fit: Slim
Coordination: -
Alternatives: Any comfy lounging pants: Moto jeggings, joggers, yoga pants. If dislike athletic look, swap for neutral ponte knit or other comfy pants with stretch.

LEGGINGS

Colors: Solid black, navy, or gray
Coordination: Used under dresses, skirts and tunics.
Alternatives: Optional to get additional pairs in other colors and/or prints.

*PRINT SKIRT

Colors: Any print in neutral, main or accent colors.
Length: Mini or knee-length recommended for option to wear with leggings + boots in fall/winter
Coordination: Color tops and color flats.
Alternatives: Midi or maxi length

BOTTOMS

*NEUTRAL SKIRT

Colors: Any solid neutral
Length: Mini or knee-length recommended for option to wear with leggings + boots in fall/winter
Coordination: -
Alternatives: Midi or maxi length

NEUTRAL SHORTS

Colors: White, black, navy, gray, rust, or khaki
Length: 3", 5", 7" or bermuda
Coordination: -
Alternatives: Neutral capri or skirt

*DENIM SHORTS

Colors: Dark, medium, or light blue denim wash
Length: 3", 5", 7" or bermuda
Coordination: -
Alternatives: Denim capri or denim skirt

*COLOR SHORTS

Colors: Spring/summer main or accent color
Length: 3", 5", 7" or bermuda
Coordination: Print tops
Alternatives: Color capri or skirt

PRINT SHORTS

Colors: Any print in main or accent spring/summer colors
Length: 3", 5", 7" or bermuda
Coordination: Color tops
Alternatives: Print capri or skirt

Finding Items In Your Price Range In some cases, the exact pieces may be from expensive sources. This is simply due to needing to find the right visuals to represent the example piece. This book comes with a Shopping Guide that offers additional shopping links for each item at various price points. Access the Shopping Guide from your dashboard. Instructions in Appendix.

COMPLETER PIECES

*DENIM JACKET

Colors: Dark, medium or light denim wash
Coordination: -
Alternatives: White denim

*SWEATSHIRT/HOODIE

Colors: Solid or print. Neutral or main/accent colors.
Coordination: Pants
Alternatives: Zip-up hoodie style

WARM PATTERN CARDIGAN

Colors: Any print in neutrals or fall/winter main colors
Style: Fitted. Hip-length or boyfriend length.
Coordination: Color tops, olive pants
Alternatives: Solid neutral or color.

*NEUTRAL LONG CARDIGAN

Colors: Solid neutral
Style: Fitted or slouchy. Boyfriend or duster length.
Coordination: -
Alternatives: Hip-length

LIGHT COLOR CARDIGAN

Colors: Light solid main or accent color
Style: Fitted or flowy. Cropped, hip-length, or boyfriend length.
Coordination: Print tops, print bottoms, print dresses
Alternatives: -

*DARK COLOR CARDIGAN

Colors: Dark solid main or accent color
Style: Fitted or flowy. Cropped, hip-length, or boyfriend length.
Coordination: Print tops, print bottoms, print dresses
Alternatives: -

KIMONO

Colors: Solid or print in neutral or main spring/summer colors
Coordination: Striped tops and dress, color tee and tanks, color bottoms
Alternatives: Used mainly in spring/summer over dresses, tees & tanks. Cool alternatives include thin or sheer pattern cardigan, bolero, short-sleeve cardigan, vest cardigan, lace cardigan.

DENIM VEST

Colors: Dark, medium, or light blue denim wash
Coordination: -
Alternatives: White denim vest

COMPLETER PIECES

*FEMININE VEST

Colors: Any neutral
Coordination: -
Alternatives: Any neutral light cover up that can be worn over dresses, tees, and tanks in summer. Crochet, lace, sheer/chiffon, or thin cotton vests. Short-sleeve cardigans.

QUILTED VEST

Colors: Any solid neutral or fall/winter main color
Coordination: Long-sleeve tops, jackets
Alternatives: Puffer vest, sweater vest, fur vest, hoodie vest, fleece vest

*UTILITY VEST

Colors: Any shade olive or other neutral such as khaki, black, gray, burgundy, or blush.
Coordination: -
Alternatives: Other commonly used terms for this kind of vest are: "military," "cargo," "army."

*PEA COAT

Colors: Any solid neutral
Coordination: -
Alternatives: Any warm winter jacket/coat. Warmer climates may find a classic "trench coat" more usable.

*UTILITY JACKET

Colors: Any shade olive or other neutral such as khaki, black, gray, burgundy, or blush.
Coordination: -
Alternatives: Other commonly used terms for this kind of jacket are: "military," "cargo," "army."

*MOTO JACKET

Colors: Any leather or solid neutral/main/accent color.
Coordination: Pants & skirts
Alternatives: Leather jacket, bomber jacket.

SHOES

*COLOR FLATS

Colors: Any solid main or accent color
Coordination: Color and print dresses and bottoms
Alternatives: Any style flats

*METALLIC FLATS

Colors: Metallic neutral
Coordination: -
Alternatives: Non-metallic solid neutral flats

Copyright © 2016-2019 Frumpy Fighters LLC   WWW.NOWTHATICANDO.COM

SHOES

PRINT FLATS

Colors: Any print in neutral, main, or accent colors
Coordination: Solid color tops, shorts, and pants
Alternatives: Floral, polka dot, geometric, gingham, other fun patterns

*THONG SANDALS

Colors: Neutral color or leather
Coordination: -
Alternatives: Also called "t-strap" sandal. Any stylish flip-flop or simple, comfy sandal.

SLIDE SANDALS

Colors: Any leather or neutral color
Coordination: -
Alternatives: Any stylish flip-flop or simple, comfy sandal.

FASHION SANDALS

Colors: Any neutral or main colors
Coordination: -
Alternatives: Any comfy but stylish sandal that makes a fun statement. Go colorful with this one if desired!

*SLIP-ON SNEAKERS

Colors: Any neutral color
Coordination: -
Alternatives: Any style fashion/casual sneaker

LACE-UP SNEAKERS

Colors: Any neutral color(s)
Coordination: -
Alternatives: Any style fashion/casual sneaker. Note: If going for an athletic sneaker, it should be a sleek, solid color. These are not meant to be workout shoes.

*RIDING BOOTS

Colors: Black, gray or brown leather
Coordination: -
Alternatives: -
Notes: Consider this an investment piece. Get genuine leather if possible to last you many years.

*ANKLE BOOTS

Colors: Any neutral genuine or faux leather/suede
Coordination: -
Alternatives: Also called "booties"

SHOES

*MOCCASIN SLIPPERS
 FW

Colors: Any neutral or main fall/winter color
Coordination: Pants
Alternatives: Any cute slipper for use around the house

ACCESSORIES

SPRING PRINT SCARF
 SS FW

Colors: Any print in neutral or spring/summer colors
Coordination: Color tops, striped tops, striped dress
Alternatives: Any light fabric with spring print

*FALL/WINTER PRINT SCARF
 FW

Colors: Any print in neutrals or fall/winter colors
Coordination: Color long-sleeve tops/sweaters
Alternatives: Any fall/winter print

*NEUTRAL SCARF
 FW

Colors: Any neutral color
Coordination: -
Alternatives: Look for thick knit. Warmer climates can skip this item or look for light fabric.

PLAID SCARF
 FW

Colors: Any plaid pattern in neutrals or fall/winter colors
Coordination: Long-sleeve tops/sweaters
Alternatives: Warmer climates can skip this item or use a plaid bandana in the hair.

*TOTE BAG
 SS FW

Colors: Any neutral or near-neutral (like chambray)
Coordination: Should coordinate with overall color scheme in both spring/summer and fall/winter
Alternatives: Any simple tote-style bag

*CROSSBODY BAG
 SS FW

Colors: Any neutral or near-neutral (like chambray)
Coordination: Should coordinate with overall color scheme in both spring/summer and fall/winter
Alternatives: Bucket or backpack bag (for ease on the playground or errands)

ACCESSORIES

*NEUTRAL BELT

Colors: Solid black or brown leather
Coordination: All bottoms and dresses
Alternatives: Any style belt, but should be able to be worn both on waist and below bustline. Look for elastic back for comfort.

COLOR BELT

Colors: Any main or accent color
Coordination: Print pieces. Bonus if complements color tops and bottoms as well.
Alternatives: Any style belt, but should be able to be worn both on waist and below bustline. Look for elastic back for comfort.

*HEADBAND

Colors: Any neutral, silver, or gold
Coordination: -
Alternatives: Elastic headband, wrap headband

BASEBALL CAP

Colors: Any neutral, denim
Coordination: -
Alternatives: Straw hat (fedora, cowgirl, panama, boat hat)

KNIT HAT

Colors: Any neutral or main fall/winter color
Coordination: Gloves, coats, jackets, utility vest, quilted vest
Alternatives: Felt or suede hat

*GLOVES

Colors: Any neutral or main fall/winter color
Coordination: Gloves, coats, jackets, utility vest, quilted vest
Alternatives: Gloves or mittens in any fabric

*CUTE SOCKS

Colors: Any colors in solid or print
Coordination: Should coordinate with fall/winter colors. Neutral socks are easiest.
Alternatives: Any ankle or no-show socks

*WOOL SOCKS

Colors: Any fall/winter colors in solid or print. At least one pair in solid neutral.
Coordination: Should coordinate with fall/winter colors. Neutral socks are easiest.
Alternatives: Warmer climates can skip

ACCESSORIES

STATEMENT EARRINGS

Colors: Solid black or brown leather
Coordination: -
Alternatives: Any fun earrings that are large or colorful.

*SIMPLE STUD EARRINGS &
*PEARL STUD EARRINGS

Colors: Neutrals/metals
Coordination: -
Alternatives: Any simple stud earrings.

STATEMENT BRACELET

Colors: Any colors or metals
Coordination: Color and print pieces
Alternatives: Metal cuff, stacked bracelet, chunky bead bracelet

MINIMALIST BRACELET

Colors: Any metals
Coordination: -
Alternatives: Charm bracelet, bangles, simple bead strand

STATEMENT NECKLACE

Colors: Any colors or metals
Coordination: Color and print tops and dresses
Alternatives: Bib necklace, bubble necklace, chunky bead strand, silicone teething necklace

*PENDANT NECKLACE

Colors: Any metal with color accents if desired
Coordination: -
Alternatives: Any medium or extra long necklace with pendant of any style

*MINIMALIST NECKLACE

Colors: Any metal
Coordination: -
Alternatives: Any delicate necklace ending above bustline

*SUNGLASSES
Colors: Neutrals
Coordination: Spring/summer tops
Alternatives: Aviators, tortoise, cat eye, circle, or sunnies

TOENAIL POLISH & *BASIC MAKEUP
- Fun toe nail color
- Foundation/BB Cream
- Mascara
- Blush
- Lip Color (LipSense recommended)

The Capsule Plan Checklist

Use the shopping checklist on the following pages to shop your closet for each item first. Essentials are marked with an asterisk (*) to make them easy to prioritize. Make notes about the items you still want to get, highlighting your top priorities.

> **Shopping Assistant Included**
>
> Want shopping links to similar options for all the pieces? This book comes with access to a supplemental shopping guide that is updated regularly and offers options from Amazon, Target, Old Navy, Nordstrom, and H&M. Also includes maternity/nursing and plus size options.
>
> See Appendix to access shopping guide.

Use the blank color palette template below to fill in the colors you want to apply to your own wardrobe pieces. This handy color scheme makes it easy to reference when you're planning and shopping!

Need help figuring out a color palette? See the *Customize Your Capsule Mini Course* in the Appendix.

My Color Palette

NEUTRAL COLORS

MAIN COLORS — spring / summer | fall / winter

ACCENT COLORS

Copyright © 2016-2019 Frumpy Fighters LLC · WWW.NOWTHATICANDO.COM

TOPS

SPRING/SUMMER	FALL/WINTER	Item	NOTES (COLOR, SLEEVE LENGTH, STYLE, ETC.)
SS	FW ❏	*Chambray Button-Down	_____
SS	FW ❏	*Short Sleeve Striped Tee	_____
	FW ❏	Long Sleeve Striped Tee	_____
SS	FW ❏	*White Basic Tee	_____
SS	FW ❏	White Fashion Tee	_____
SS	FW ❏	*Gray Tee	_____
	FW ❏	*Long Sleeve Navy Tee	_____
SS	FW ❏	Color Tee	_____
SS	FW ❏	*Print Tee #1	_____
SS	FW ❏	Print Tee #2	_____
SS	FW ❏	*Color Sleeveless Top #1	_____
SS	FW ❏	Color Sleeveless Top #2	_____
SS	FW ❏	Print Sleeveless Top #1	_____
SS	FW ❏	Print Sleeveless Top #2	_____
SS	FW ❏	*Neutral Fitted Tank	_____
SS	FW ❏	*Neutral Tunic Top	_____
SS	FW ❏	Graphic Tee	_____
SS	FW ❏	Slogan Tee	_____
SS	FW ❏	Color Dressy Top	_____
SS	FW ❏	*Neutral Dressy Top	_____
SS	FW ❏	Print Dressy Top	_____
	FW ❏	*Neutral Plaid Button-Down	_____
	FW ❏	Color Plaid Button-Down	_____
	FW ❏	*Color Fitted Sweater	_____
	FW ❏	Neutral Slouchy Sweater	_____
	FW ❏	*Neutral Tunic Sweater	_____

Copyright © 2016-2019 Frumpy Fighters LLC — WWW.NOWTHATICANDO.COM

NOTES (COLOR, STYLE, ETC.)

DRESSES

SS	FW	❏	Print Knee-length Dress	_____
SS	FW	❏	Chambray Dress	_____
SS	FW	❏	*Neutral Knee-length Dress	_____
SS	FW	❏	*Striped Dress	_____
SS	FW	❏	*Black Maxi Dress	_____

BOTTOMS

SS	FW	❏	*Dark Wash Jeans	_____
SS	FW	❏	Light Wash Jeans	_____
SS	FW	❏	*Neutral Jeans	_____
SS	FW	❏	*Olive Pants	_____
SS	FW	❏	Color Pants	_____
	FW	❏	Slim Fit Athletic Pants	_____
	FW	❏	Leggings	_____
SS	FW	❏	*Print Skirt	_____
SS	FW	❏	*Neutral Skirt	_____
SS		❏	Neutral Shorts	_____
SS		❏	*Denim Shorts	_____
SS		❏	*Color Shorts	_____
SS		❏	Print Shorts	_____

NOTES (COLOR, STYLE, ETC.)

COMPLETER PIECES

SS	FW	☐	*Denim Jacket
	FW	☐	*Sweatshirt/Hoodie
	FW	☐	Warm Pattern Cardigan
SS	FW	☐	*Neutral Long Cardigan
SS	FW	☐	Light Color Cardigan
SS	FW	☐	* Dark Color Cardigan
SS		☐	Kimono
SS		☐	Denim Vest
SS	FW	☐	*Feminine Vest
	FW	☐	Quilted Vest
SS	FW	☐	*Utility Vest
	FW	☐	*Pea Coat
SS	FW	☐	*Utility Jacket
SS	FW	☐	*Moto Jacket

SHOES

SS	FW	☐	*Color Flats
SS	FW	☐	*Metallic Flats
SS	FW	☐	Print Flats
SS		☐	*Thong Sandals
SS		☐	Slide Sandals
SS	FW	☐	Fashion Sandals
SS	FW	☐	*Slip-On Sneakers
SS	FW	☐	Lace-Up Sneakers
	FW	☐	*Riding Boots
	FW	☐	*Ankle Boots
	FW	☐	*Moccasin Slippers

Copyright © 2016-2019 Frumpy Fighters LLC   WWW.NOWTHATICANDO.COM

ACCESSORIES

NOTES (COLOR, STYLE, ETC.)

			Item	Notes
SS	FW	☐	Spring Print Scarf	_____
	FW	☐	*Fall/Winter Print Scarf	_____
	FW	☐	*Neutral Scarf	_____
	FW	☐	Plaid Scarf	_____
SS	FW	☐	*Tote Bag	_____
SS	FW	☐	*Crossbody Bag	_____
SS	FW	☐	*Neutral Belt	_____
SS	FW	☐	Color Belt	_____
SS	FW	☐	*Headband	_____
SS		☐	Baseball Cap	_____
	FW	☐	Knit Hat	_____
	FW	☐	*Gloves	_____
SS	FW	☐	*Cute Socks	_____
	FW	☐	*Wool Socks	_____
SS	FW	☐	Statement Earrings	_____
SS	FW	☐	*Pearl Stud Earrings	_____
SS	FW	☐	*Simple Stud Earrings	_____
SS	FW	☐	Statement Bracelet	_____
SS	FW	☐	Minimalist Bracelet	_____
SS	FW	☐	Statement Necklace	_____
SS	FW	☐	*Pendant Necklace	_____
SS	FW	☐	*Minimalist Necklace	_____
SS	FW	☐	*Sunglasses	_____
SS	FW	☐	Toe Nail Polish	_____
SS	FW	☐	*Basic Makeup	_____

SPRING/ SUMMER	FALL/ WINTER		NOTES (COLOR, SLEEVE LENGTH, STYLE, ETC.)

OTHER

Part 3:

The Outfits

The Outfit Gallery Web App:
Browse the Outfits Online

You can also browse the entire library of outfits on the outfit gallery web app. The web app allows you to sort outfits by specific clothing pieces and jump to different seasons easily.

You can save a shortcut to the gallery on your phone and flip through outfits easily to choose one for the day.

Access via your dashboard. See Appendix for instructions.

How to View the Outfits on Real People:
Frump Fighters Facebook Group

Need to see an outfit on a real person? Join the private Facebook group to see these outfits worn by other moms! Use the search box within the group to search for an outfit number. Outfits from this guide are sometimes also referred to as FYW (full year wardrobe) or YRW (year round wardrobe). Note: Some outfits that are shared may be from a different outfit guide such as one of the single-season guides. They are usually labeled as such.

Join the Frump Fighters Facebook group at www.nowthaticando.com/facebook-group

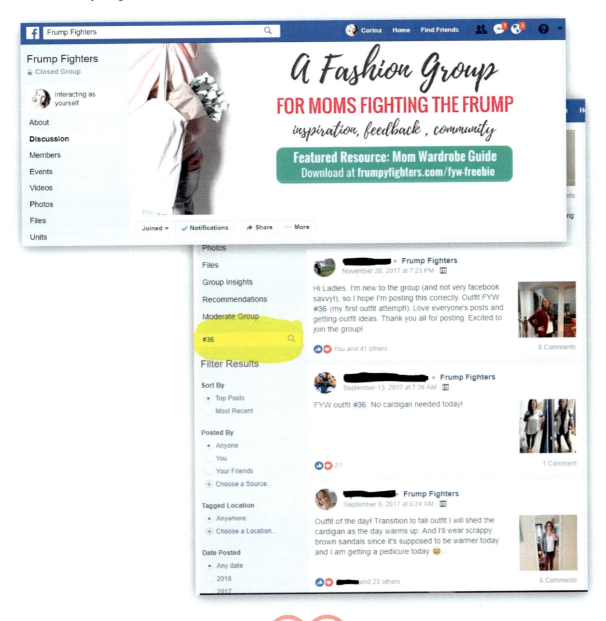

How To Read The Outfit Pages

In this section there are about 60 casual outfits and 10 dressy outfits per season, totaling 288 outfits. They are arranged in this order:

Outfits 1-51: Casual Outfits for Fall
Outfits 52-61: Dressy Outfits for Fall
Outfits 62-105: Casual Outfits for Winter
Outfits 106-115: Dressy Outfits for Winter
Outfits 116-168: Casual Outfits for Spring
Outfits 169-178: Dressy Outfits for Spring
Outfits 179-229: Casual Outfits for Summer
Outfits 230-239: Dressy Outfits for Summer

The 288 outfits in this section represent *all* the possible ways to combine your base pieces (*tops + bottoms* or *dresses + completer pieces*).

All the possible outfit combinations are spread out over the four seasons without any repeats. When you've worked through the combinations in this book, you know you've truly maximized the use of your wardrobe.

Because there are no repeating outfits, it's easy to create even more variation by simply taking the top and bottom or dress from one outfit and accessorizing it differently to work in another season. In other words, 288 outfits is just the beginning!

Simply work your way through the outfit numbers one day at a time and change things up as you desire.

On the next page, I'll explain how to "read" the outfit visual pages.

The NEW Outfits
If you've purchased the previous version of this guide, you are probably looking for the new outfits! There are 3 ways to find these easily:
1. Look for the "a" after an outfit number in this eBook.
2. Go on the outfit gallery web app and click on link to view just new outfits.
3. Download the PDF of just the new outfits (On your dashboard. Access via [Appendix](#)).

Color-coded side bars lengthen with each season. On the printed guide these can be used as tabs when flipping through your book.

If you print your guide, you can use these checkmark circles to keep track of what you've tried. There's enough room to even write in the date it was worn if you wish!

Keep track of which outfits you're looking at with these handy headers.

OUTFITS 62-105: WINTER CASUAL

Outfit #85a

Neutral Plaid Button-Down
+ Dark Wash Jeans
+ Color Fitted Sweater
+ Cute Socks
+ Pendant Necklace
+ Quilted Vest
+ Gloves
+ Spring Print Scarf
+ Crossbody Bag
+ Ankle Boots

Outfits that are new to this version are labeled with an "a" after the outfit number

Sweater over button-down. Fold button-down's cuffs up over sweater sleeves once or twice.
Roll pant hems 1-2" to wear with ankle boots.

Outfit #86

Print Sleeveless Top #1
+ Dark Wash Jeans
+ Dark Color Cardigan
+ Wool Socks
+ Statement Earrings
+ Color Belt
+ Pea Coat
+ Gloves
+ Fall/Winter Print Scarf
+ Tote Bag
+ Print Flats

Visuals help you see the "big picture" while the written outfit formulas helps you recreate the outfit with your pieces.

Belt in belt loops. Optional partial front tuck.

81

If you print your outfit sheets, you can use the dotted line to cut the sheets in half and place them on a metal ring as outfit cards.

Stylist notes provide additional guidance for putting outfits together.

The left section tells you what to wear while home.

The right column indicates what you would add when you go out.

Copyright © 2016-2019 Frumpy Fighters LLC   37   WWW.NOWTHATICANDO.COM

Casual Outfits for Fall
Outfits 1-51

OUTFITS 1-51: FALL CASUAL

○ ○ ○ ○ ○

Outfit #1

Long Sleeve Navy Tee
+ Color Shorts
+ Spring Print Scarf
+ Pearl Stud Earrings
+ Minimalist Bracelet
+ Denim Vest
+ Crossbody Bag
+ Print Flats

For early fall.

○ ○ ○ ○ ○

Outfit #2

Color Plaid Button-Down
+ White Basic Tee
+ Denim Shorts
+ Color Belt
+ Pearl Stud Earrings
+ Dark Color Cardigan
+ Crossbody Bag
+ Slip-On Sneakers

OUTFITS 1-51: FALL CASUAL

Outfit #3

Neutral Plaid Button-Down
+ Color Tee
+ Neutral Skirt
+ Simple Stud Earrings
+ Headband
+ Moto Jacket
+ Tote Bag
+ Riding Boots

Wear plaid button-down over color tee. If your tee has a twist like the exact one, wear open or buttoned from chest-level down. Partial tuck optional. If tee doesn't have bottom hem detail, try tucking color tee into skirt and wearing button-down open with bottom ends tied.

Outfit #3a

Neutral Plaid Button-Down
+ Basic White Tee
+ Color Shorts
+ Pearl Stud Earrings
+ Denim Jacket
+ Crossbody Bag
+ Metallic Flats

For early fall. Wear plaid button-down over white tee; can be closed, open, or partially buttoned with bottom ends tied.

OUTFITS 1-51: FALL CASUAL

Outfit #4

Graphic Tee
+ Olive Pants
+ Warm Pattern Cardigan
+ Statement Earrings
+ Cute Socks
+ Moto Jacket
+ Crossbody Bag
+ Lace-up Sneakers

Swap long cardigan for moto jacket when going out.

Outfit #4a

Color Plaid Button-Down
+ Neutral Shorts
+ Headband
+ Pendant Necklace
+ Neutral Belt
+ Utility Vest
+ Tote Bag
+ Thong Sandals

For early fall. Belt at waist. Optional partial front tuck.

OUTFITS 1-51: FALL CASUAL

Outfit #5

White Basic Tee
+ Olive Pants
+ Warm Pattern Cardigan
+ Simple Stud Earrings
+ Minimalist Necklace
+ Moccasin Slippers
+ Crossbody Bag
+ Lace-up Sneakers

Outfit #6

Neutral Plaid Button-Down
+ Neutral Fitted Tank
+ Neutral Jeans
+ Pearl Stud Earrings
+ Moccasin Slippers
+ Quilted Vest
+ Tote Bag
+ Metallic Flats

Wear plaid button-down over tank; can be closed, open, or partially buttoned with bottom ends tied.

OUTFITS 1-51: FALL CASUAL

Outfit #7

Neutral Tunic Top
+ Light Wash Jeans
+ Warm Pattern Cardigan
+ Statement Bracelet
+ Pendant Necklace
+ Cute Socks
+ Neutral Scarf
+ Crossbody Bag
+ Metallic Flats

Outfit #7a

Chambray Dress
+ Dark Color Cardigan
+ Pearl Stud Earrings
+ Minimalist Bracelet
+ Spring Print Scarf
+ Tote Bag
+ Riding Boots

OUTFITS 1-51: FALL CASUAL

Partial tuck.

Outfit #8

Short Sleeve Striped Tee
+ Slim Fit Athletic Pants
+ Light Color Cardigan
+ Simple Stud Earrings
+ Headband
+ Cute Socks
+ Utility Jacket
+ Crossbody Bag
+ Lace-up Sneakers

Outfit #9

Color Sleeveless Top #1
+ Dark Wash Jeans
+ Warm Pattern Cardigan
+ Pearl Stud Earrings
+ Pendant Necklace
+ Moccasin Slippers
+ Tote Bag
+ Riding Boots

OUTFITS 1-51: FALL CASUAL

Outfit # 10

Neutral Knee-Length Dress
+ Denim Jacket
+ Pendant Necklace
+ Minimalist Bracelet
+ Moccasin Slippers
+ Fall/Winter Print Scarf
+ Tote Bag
+ Ankle Boots

Outfit #11

Short Sleeve Striped Tee
+ Light Wash Jeans
+ Fall/Winter Print Scarf
+ Simple Stud Earrings
+ Minimalist Bracelet
+ Moccasin Slippers
+ Utility Jacket
+ Crossbody Bag
+ Lace-up Sneakers

Optional partial front tuck.

OUTFITS 1-51: FALL CASUAL

Outfit #12

Gray Tee
+ Olive Pants
+ Neutral Scarf
+ Simple Stud Earrings
+ Moccasin Slippers
+ Sweatshirt/Hoodie
+ Crossbody Bag
+ Slip-on Sneakers

Optional partial front tuck.

Outfit #13

Print Tee #1
+ Slim Fit Athletic Pants
+ Dark Color Cardigan
+ Pearl Stud Earrings
+ Minimalist Necklace
+ Cute Socks
+ Denim Jacket
+ Crossbody Bag
+ Slip-on Sneakers

Optional: Swap long cardigan for denim jacket when going out.

OUTFITS 1-51: FALL CASUAL

Outfit #13a

Black Maxi Dress
+ Color Plaid Button-Down
+ Pearl Stud Earrings
+ Minimalist Bracelet
+ Denim Jacket
+ Tote Bag
+ Thong Sandals

Wear plaid button-down with bottom ends tied.

Outfit #14

Print Tee #2
+ Olive Pants
+ Neutral Long Cardigan
+ Statement Earrings
+ Wool Socks
+ Denim Jacket
+ Tote Bag
+ Ankle Boots

When going out either swap cardigan with jacket or layer. Roll 1-2" pant cuff to wear with ankle boots. Optional: Partial tuck.

OUTFITS 1-51: FALL CASUAL

○ ○ ○ ○ ○

Outfit #15

Chambray Button-Down
+ Short Sleeve Striped Tee
+ Olive Pants
+ Minimalist Necklace
+ Minimalist Bracelet
+ Cute Socks
+ Moto Jacket
+ Fall/Winter Print Scarf
+ Crossbody Bag
+ Metallic Flats

Layer Chambray over tee either open or partially buttoned with ends tied. If tie ends then tuck in striped tee and consider adding neutral belt. Remove socks to go out.

○ ○ ○ ○ ○

Outfit #16

Long Sleeve Navy Tee
+ Light Wash Jeans
+ Plaid Scarf
+ Statement Bracelet
+ Headband
+ Moccasin Slippers
+ Utility Vest
+ Tote Bag
+ Slip-on Sneakers

If shirt is not fitted, do a partial front tuck.

OUTFITS 1-51: FALL CASUAL

Outfit #17

Print Tee #2
+ Slim Fit Athletic Pants
+ Light Color Cardigan
+ Simple Stud Earrings
+ Cute Socks
+ Neutral Scarf
+ Crossbody Bag
+ Lace-up Sneakers

Optional: Partial tuck.

Outfit #18

Print Sleeveless Top #1
+ Olive Pants
+ Light Color Cardigan
+ Pearl Stud Earrings
+ Minimalist Bracelet
+ Moccasin Slippers
+ Moto Jacket
+ Tote Bag
+ Metallic Flats

When going out either swap cardigan with jacket or layer.

49

OUTFITS 1-51: FALL CASUAL

Outfit #18a

Neutral Tunic Top
+ Color Pants
+ Plaid Scarf
+ Simple Stud Earrings
+ Pendant Necklace
+ Wool Socks
+ Utility Jacket
+ Tote Bag
+ Metallic Flats

Outfit #19

Print Sleeveless Top #1
+ Light Wash Jeans
+ Dark Color Cardigan
+ Statement Earrings
+ Moccasin Slippers
+ Utility Jacket
+ Spring Print Scarf
+ Tote Bag
+ Ankle Boots

Roll pant hems 1-2" to wear with ankle boots.

OUTFITS 1-51: FALL CASUAL

Outfit #20

Slogan Tee
+ Olive Pants
+ Headband
+ Minimalist Necklace
+ Cute Socks
+ Denim Jacket
+ Crossbody Bag
+ Slip-on Sneakers

Optional partial front tuck. When going out either swap cardigan with jacket or layer.

Outfit #20a

Chambray Button-Down
+ Neutral Slouchy Sweater
+ Olive Pants
+ Pearl Stud Earrings
+ Minimalist Necklace
+ Wool Socks
+ Fall/Winter Print Scarf
+ Crossbody Bag
+ Ankle Boots

Wear chambray button-down under slouchy sweater. Fold cuffs up once over sweater sleeves. Roll pant hems 1-2" to wear with ankle boots.

OUTFITS 1-51: FALL CASUAL

Outfit #21

Striped Dress
+ Denim Jacket
+ Pearl Stud Earrings
+ Statement Necklace
+ Moccasin Slippers
+ Fall/Winter Print Scarf
+ Tote Bag
+ Riding Boots

Outfit #22

Print Tee #2
+ Dark Wash Jeans
+ Dark Color Cardigan
+ Color Belt
+ Simple Stud Earrings
+ Cute Socks
+ Neutral Scarf
+ Tote Bag
+ Color Flats

Belt in belt loops. Partial tuck. Swap socks for flats when going out.

OUTFITS 1-51: FALL CASUAL

Outfit #23

Neutral Slouchy Sweater
+ Light Wash Jeans
+ Plaid Scarf
+ Statement Earrings
+ Minimalist Bracelet
+ Cute Socks
+ Quilted Vest
+ Crossbody Bag
+ Metallic Flats

Optional partial front tuck.

Outfit #24

Color Tee
+ Slim Fit Athletic Pants
+ Warm Pattern Cardigan
+ Simple Stud Earrings
+ Pendant Necklace
+ Moccasin Slippers
+ Neutral Scarf
+ Crossbody Bag
+ Lace-up Sneakers

OUTFITS 1-51: FALL CASUAL

Outfit #25

Color Plaid Button-Down
+ Neutral Jeans
+ Statement Necklace
+ Minimalist Bracelet
+ Cute Socks
+ Quilted Vest
+ Neutral Scarf
+ Tote Bag
+ Ankle Boots

Roll 1-2" cuff on pants to wear with ankle boots.

Outfit #25a

Black Maxi Dress
+ Utility Vest
+ Statement Earrings
+ Minimalist Necklace
+ Cute Socks
+ Fall/Winter Print Scarf
+ Crossbody Bag
+ Fashion Sandals

OUTFITS 1-51: FALL CASUAL

○ ○ ○ ○ ○

Outfit #26

Striped Dress
+ Neutral Belt
+ Denim Vest
+ Statement Earrings
+ Moccasin Slippers
+ Utility Jacket
+ Neutral Scarf
+ Crossbody Bag
+ Color Flats

If your dress is short sleeve, layer with cardigan or swap with denim jacket.

○ ○ ○ ○ ○

Outfit #27

Print Sleeveless Top #2
+ Dark Wash Jeans
+ Dark Color Cardigan
+ Simple Stud Earrings
+ Statement Bracelet
+ Neutral Belt
+ Moccasin Slippers
+ Moto Jacket
+ Tote Bag
+ Ankle Boots

Belt in belt loops. Optional front tuck.
Roll pant hems 1-2" to wear with ankle boots.

OUTFITS 1-51: FALL CASUAL

Outfit #28

Long Sleeve Striped Tee
+ Olive Pants
+ Pearl Stud Earrings
+ Minimalist Bracelet
+ Wool Socks
+ Quilted Vest
+ Fall/Winter Print Scarf
+ Tote Bag
+ Riding Boots

Partial tuck.

Outfit #29

Gray Tee
+ Slim Fit Athletic Pants
+ Denim Jacket
+ Pearl Stud Earrings
+ Pendant Necklace
+ Cute Socks
+ Plaid Scarf
+ Crossbody Bag
+ Slip-on Sneakers

OUTFITS 1-51: FALL CASUAL

Outfit #29a

Color Plaid Button-Down
+ White Basic Tee
+ Color Pants
+ Statement Earrings
+ Wool Socks
+ Neutral Long Cardigan
+ Tote Bag
+ Riding Boots

Wear plaid button-down over white tee. Can be closed, open, or partially buttoned with bottom ends tied. The color plaid with color pants may or may not work depending on colors in your plaid.

Outfit #30

Striped Dress
+ Leggings
+ Minimalist Necklace
+ Minimalist Bracelet
+ Wool Socks
+ Utility Vest
+ Plaid Scarf
+ Tote Bag
+ Riding Boots

If your dress is short sleeve, layer with cardigan first.

OUTFITS 1-51: FALL CASUAL

When going out either swap leather jacket or just wear utility vest and add any scarf for warmth.

Outfit #31

Long Sleeve Striped Tee
+ Neutral Skirt
+ Utility Vest
+ Statement Necklace
+ Moccasin Slippers
+ Moto Jacket
+ Tote Bag
+ Metallic Flats

If shirt is not fitted, do a partial front tuck.

Outfit #32

Long Sleeve Navy Tee
+ Print Skirt
+ Leggings
+ Statement Earrings
+ Statement Bracelet
+ Moccasin Slippers
+ Denim Vest
+ Neutral Scarf
+ Crossbody Bag
+ Riding Boots

OUTFITS 1-51: FALL CASUAL

Outfit #33

Print Tee #1
+ Light Wash Jeans
+ Dark Color Cardigan
+ Pearl Stud Earrings
+ Moccasin Slippers
+ Utility Vest
+ Tote Bag
+ Metallic Flats

When going out add utility vest over cardigan.

Outfit #34

Print Sleeveless Top #2
+ Neutral Jeans
+ Neutral Scarf
+ Statement Earrings
+ Wool Socks
+ Sweatshirt/Hoodie
+ Crossbody Bag
+ Slip-on Sneakers

OUTFITS 1-51: FALL CASUAL

Outfit #35

Chambray Dress
+ Neutral Belt
+ Utility Vest
+ Simple Stud Earrings
+ Moccasin Slippers
+ Fall/Winter Print Scarf
+ Tote Bag
+ Ankle Boots

Optional: Add leggings for warmth.

Outfit #35a

Long Sleeve Navy Tee
+ Color Pants
+ Feminine Vest
+ Statement Necklace
+ Cute Socks
+ Utility Jacket
+ Plaid Scarf
+ Crossbody Bag
+ Ankle Boots

Roll pant hems 1-2" to wear with ankle boots.

OUTFITS 1-51: FALL CASUAL

Outfit #36

White Fashion Tee
+ Olive Pants
+ Statement Earrings
+ Pendant Necklace
+ Neutral Long Cardigan
+ Cute Socks
+ Fall/Winter Print Scarf
+ Tote Bag
+ Riding Boots

If pants are not skinny fit, swap for ankle boots and roll 1-2" cuff on pants to wear with ankle boots.

Outfit #37

Color Fitted Sweater
+ Print Skirt
+ Pearl Stud Earrings
+ Minimalist Necklace
+ Moccasin Slippers
+ Denim Jacket
+ Tote Bag
+ Metallic Flats

OUTFITS 1-51: FALL CASUAL

Outfit #38

Color Plaid Button-Down
+ Neutral Fitted Tank
+ Olive Pants
+ Simple Stud Earrings
+ Neutral Belt
+ Wool Socks
+ Quilted Vest
+ Crossbody Bag
+ Lace-up Sneakers

Belt in belt loops. Layer button-down over tank either open, partially open, or partially buttoned with ends tied. If partially open, do a partial front tuck.

Outfit #39

Neutral Knee-Length Dress
+ Neutral Plaid Button-Down
+ Pearl Stud Earrings
+ Moccasin Slippers
+ Denim Vest
+ Neutral Scarf
+ Crossbody Bag
+ Riding Boots

Wear button-down closed or bottom ends tied. If closed, optionally add neutral belt at natural waist. Add leggings for warmth.

OUTFITS 1-51: FALL CASUAL

Outfit #40

Neutral Plaid Button-Down
+ Light Wash Jeans
+ Color Fitted Sweater
+ Pearl Stud Earrings
+ Cute Socks
+ Moto Jacket
+ Tote Bag
+ Metallic Flats

Wear button-up under sweater with sleeves and collar poking out.

Outfit #41

Graphic Tee
+ Slim Fit Athletic Pants
+ Dark Color Cardigan
+ Simple Stud Earrings
+ Minimalist Necklace
+ Cute Socks
+ Utility Jacket
+ Crossbody Bag
+ Slip-on Sneakers

Partial tuck.

OUTFITS 1-51: FALL CASUAL

Outfit #42

Neutral Tunic Top
+ Neutral Jeans
+ Warm Pattern Cardigan
+ Statement Earrings
+ Pendant Necklace
+ Moccasin Slippers
+ Utility Jacket
+ Tote Bag
+ Print Flats

Outfit #43

Print Dressy Top
+ Light Wash Jeans
+ Neutral Long Cardigan
+ Neutral Belt
+ Pearl Stud Earrings
+ Headband
+ Moccasin Slippers
+ Moto Jacket
+ Neutral Scarf
+ Tote Bag
+ Color Flats

Belt in belt loops.

OUTFITS 1-51: FALL CASUAL

Outfit #44

White Basic Tee
+ Dark Wash Jeans
+ Warm Pattern Cardigan
+ Statement Necklace
+ Color Belt
+ Wool Socks
+ Utility Jacket
+ Crossbody Bag
+ Riding Boots

Belt in loops. Partial tuck.

Outfit #45

Neutral Tunic Top
+ Leggings
+ Fall/Winter Print Scarf
+ Statement Earrings
+ Wool Socks
+ Utility Jacket
+ Crossbody Bag
+ Riding Boots

OUTFITS 1-51: FALL CASUAL

Button-down open or partially buttoned and bottom ends tied. Can also button completely and add a belt at waist.
Optional: Add leggings for warmth.

Outfit #46

Print Knee-Length Dress
+ Chambray Button-Down
+ Pearl Stud Earrings
+ Minimalist Necklace
+ Wool Socks
+ Light Color Cardigan
+ Neutral Scarf
+ Tote Bag
+ Ankle Boots

Outfit #46a

Long Sleeve Striped Tee
+ Color Pants
+ Headband
+ Minimalist Bracelet
+ Moccasin Slippers
+ Utility Vest
+ Spring Print Scarf
+ Crossbody Bag
+ Metallic Flats

OUTFITS 1-51: FALL CASUAL

Outfit #47

Neutral Plaid Button-Down
+ Neutral Knee-Length Skirt
+ Gray Tee
+ Simple Stud Earrings
+ Moccasin Slippers
+ Denim Jacket
+ Neutral Scarf
+ Tote Bag
+ Metallic Flats

Tee under plaid top completely tucked. Plaid top buttoned from bust down, with partial front tuck. For warmth, add leggings and swap flats with riding boots.

Outfit #48

Long Sleeve Striped Tee
+ Light Wash Jeans
+ Fall/Winter Print Scarf
+ Statement Earrings
+ Neutral Belt
+ Moccasin Slippers
+ Utility Vest
+ Tote Bag
+ Ankle Boots

Belt in belt loops. Partial tuck.
Roll pant hems 1-2" to wear with ankle boots.

OUTFITS 1-51: FALL CASUAL

Outfit #49

Chambray Dress
+ Neutral Long Cardigan
+ Leggings
+ Pearl Stud Earrings
+ Headband
+ Moccasin Slippers
+ Plaid Scarf
+ Tote Bag
+ Riding Boots

If your chambray dress is long-sleeve shirt dress, unbutton cuffs and fold back over cardigan sleeve.

Outfit #50

White Basic Tee
+ Slim Fit Athletic Pants
+ Neutral Long Cardigan
+ Minimalist Necklace
+ Minimalist Bracelet
+ Cute Socks
+ Utility Jacket
+ Knit Hat
+ Crossbody Bag
+ Lace-up Sneakers

Partial front tuck.

OUTFITS 1-51: FALL CASUAL

Outfit #50a

Black Maxi Dress
+ Chambray Button-Down
+ Wool Socks
+ Headband
+ Statement Necklace
+ Quilted Vest
+ Tote Bag
+ Metallic Flats

Wear chambray over dress, buttoned top to bottom.
Leave last one or two buttons undone and tie the ends.
Statement necklace over buttoned chambray, tucked under collar.

Outfit #51

Neutral Tunic Sweater
+ Light Wash Jeans
+ Utility Vest
+ Simple Stud Earrings
+ Moccasin Slippers
+ Fall/Winter Print Scarf
+ Tote Bag
+ Slip-on Sneakers

Dressy Outfits for Fall
Outfits 52-61

OUTFITS 52-61: FALL DRESSY

Outfit #52

Print Dressy Top
+ Olive Pants
+ Neutral Long Cardigan
+ Statement Earrings
+ Pendant Necklace
+ Neutral Scarf
+ Tote Bag
+ Metallic Flats

Outfit #53

Neutral Tunic Top
+ Dark Wash Jeans
+ Moto Jacket
+ Pearl Stud Earrings
+ Pendant Necklace
+ Fall/Winter Print Scarf
+ Tote Bag
+ Ankle Boots

Roll pant hems 1-2" to wear with ankle boots.

OUTFITS 52-61: FALL DRESSY

Outfit #54

Striped Dress
+ Feminine Vest
+ Simple Stud Earrings
+ Neutral Belt
+ Fall/Winter Print Scarf
+ Tote Bag
+ Color Flats

Belt over dress (under vest) at natural waist. If dress is short sleeve or tank, swap vest with cardigan or jacket.

Outfit #55

Neutral Dressy Top
+ Dark Wash Jeans
+ Dark Color Cardigan
+ Statement Earrings
+ Minimalist Necklace
+ Spring Print Scarf
+ Tote Bag
+ Print Flats

OUTFITS 52-61: FALL DRESSY

Outfit #56

Chambray Button-Down
+ Neutral Skirt
+ Feminine Vest
+ Pearl Stud Earrings
+ Statement Necklace
+ Neutral Belt
+ Tote Bag
+ Riding Boots

Outfit #57

Color Dressy Top
+ Leggings
+ Neutral Long Cardigan
+ Statement Earrings
+ Pendant Necklace
+ Fall/Winter Print Scarf
+ Tote Bag
+ Riding Boots

Can sub in tunic top if dressy top doesn't cover the bum.

OUTFITS 52-61: FALL DRESSY

○ ○ ○ ○ ○

Outfit #58

Print Dressy Top
+ Dark Wash Jeans
+ Moto Jacket
+ Simple Stud Earrings
+ Statement Necklace
+ Neutral Belt
+ Tote Bag
+ Ankle Boots

Belt in belt loops. Roll pant hems 1-2" to wear with ankle boots.

○ ○ ○ ○ ○

Outfit #59

Print Knee-Length Dress
+ Long Sleeve Navy Tee
+ Statement Earrings
+ Statement Bracelet
+ Denim Vest
+ Tote Bag
+ Color Flats

Tee over dress and denim vest over tee.

74

OUTFITS 52-61: FALL DRESSY

Outfit #60

Print Dressy Top
+ Neutral Jeans
+ Moto Jacket
+ Pearl Stud Earrings
+ Statement Bracelet
+ Tote Bag
+ Metallic Flats

Outfit #61

Striped Dress
+ Dark Color Cardigan
+ Color Belt
+ Pearl Stud Earrings
+ Minimalist Necklace
+ Tote Bag
+ Metallic Flats

Belt at natural waist either under or over cardigan.

Casual Outfits for Winter
Outfits 62-105

OUTFITS 62-105: WINTER CASUAL

Outfit #62

Gray Tee
+ Neutral Jeans
+ Warm Pattern Cardigan
+ Statement Earrings
+ Wool Socks
+ Utility Jacket
+ Gloves
+ Knit Hat
+ Crossbody Bag
+ Riding Boots

Slouchy sweater over dress.

Outfit #63

Neutral Knee-Length Dress
+ Neutral Slouchy Sweater
+ Leggings
+ Wool Socks
+ Minimalist Necklace
+ Headband
+ Pea Coat
+ Fall/Winter Print Scarf
+ Tote Bag
+ Riding Boots

OUTFITS 62-105: WINTER CASUAL

Outfit #64

Neutral Plaid Button-Down
+ Long Sleeve Navy Tee
+ Slim Fit Athletic Pants
+ Cute Socks
+ Simple Stud Earrings
+ Neutral Scarf
+ Utility Jacket
+ Crossbody Bag
+ Knit Hat
+ Lace-Up Sneakers

Button-down over tee, open or buttoned.

Outfit #64a

Print Knee-Length Dress
+ Dark Color Cardigan
+ Leggings
+ Moccasin Slippers
+ Statement Earrings
+ Minimalist Bracelet
+ Moto Jacket
+ Neutral Scarf
+ Tote Bag
+ Riding Boots

OUTFITS 62-105: WINTER CASUAL

Outfit #65

Neutral Plaid Button-Down
+ Long Sleeve Navy Tee
+ Olive Pants
+ Wool Socks
+ Pendant Necklace
+ Minimalist Bracelet
+ Pea Coat
+ Knit Hat
+ Tote Bag
+ Ankle Boots

Button-down over tee, open or buttoned.
Roll pant hems 1-2" to wear with ankle boots.

Outfit #66

Striped Dress
+ Color Fitted Sweater
+ Leggings
+ Wool Socks
+ Pendant Necklace
+ Fall/Winter Print Scarf
+ Pea Coat
+ Crossbody Bag
+ Gloves
+ Riding Boots

Sweater over dress.

Optional partial tuck.

Outfit #67

Print Sleeveless Top #2
+ Olive Pants
+ Neutral Long Cardigan
+ Cute Socks
+ Headband
+ Pearl Stud Earrings
+ Pea Coat
+ Gloves
+ Neutral Scarf
+ Tote Bag
+ Riding Boots

Outfit #68

Long Sleeve Navy Tee
+ Slim Fit Athletic Pants
+ Sweatshirt/Hoodie
+ Moccasin Slippers
+ Simple Stud Earrings
+ Headband
+ Quilted Vest
+ Knit Hat
+ Crossbody Bag
+ Slip-On Sneakers

OUTFITS 62-105: WINTER CASUAL

Outfit #68a

Neutral Plaid Button-Down
+ Color Pants
+ Utility Vest
+ Cute Socks
+ Simple Stud Earrings
+ Pea Coat
+ Knit Hat
+ Gloves
+ Crossbody Bag
+ Slip-On Sneakers

Outfit #69

Long Sleeve Navy Tee
+ Olive Pants
+ Quilted Vest
+ Wool Socks
+ Statement Earrings
+ Moto Jacket
+ Neutral Scarf
+ Knit Hat
+ Crossbody Bag
+ Ankle Boots

Roll pant hems 1-2" to wear with ankle boots.

OUTFITS 62-105: WINTER CASUAL

Belt in belt loops. Optional partial tuck.

Outfit #70

Color Plaid Button-Down
+ Dark Wash Jeans
+ Utility Vest
+ Moccasin Slippers
+ Neutral Belt
+ Statement Bracelet
+ Pearl Stud Earrings
+ Pea Coat
+ Neutral Scarf
+ Knit Hat
+ Tote Bag
+ Riding Boots

Outfit #70a

Black Maxi Dress
+ Neutral Long Cardigan
+ Moccasin Slippers
+ Fall/Winter Print Scarf
+ Pearl Stud Earrings
+ Pea Coat
+ Knit Hat
+ Gloves
+ Tote Bag
+ Riding Boots

OUTFITS 62-105: WINTER CASUAL

Outfit #71

Slogan Tee
+ Dark Wash Jeans
+ Dark Color Cardigan
+ Cute Socks
+ Headband
+ Statement Earrings
+ Pea Coat
+ Spring Print Scarf
+ Gloves
+ Crossbody Bag
+ Lace-Up Sneakers

Outfit #72

Neutral Tunic Sweater
+ Neutral Jeans
+ Quilted Vest
+ Cute Socks
+ Simple Stud Earrings
+ Plaid Scarf
+ Utility Jacket
+ Knit Hat
+ Tote Bag
+ Ankle Boots

Roll pant hems 1-2" to wear with ankle boots.

OUTFITS 62-105: WINTER CASUAL

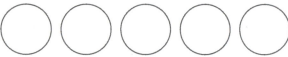

Outfit #73

Chambray Dress
+ Warm Pattern Cardigan
+ Leggings
+ Wool Socks
+ Statement Earrings
+ Utility Jacket
+ Neutral Scarf
+ Gloves
+ Tote Bag
+ Riding Boots

Outfit #74

Color Fitted Sweater
+ Dark Wash Jeans
+ Quilted Vest
+ Wool Socks
+ Plaid Scarf
+ Pearl Stud Earrings
+ Moto Jacket
+ Tote Bag
+ Gloves
+ Slip-On Sneakers

OUTFITS 62-105: WINTER CASUAL

Outfit #74a

Neutral Slouchy Sweater
+ Color Pants
+ Moccasins
+ Pendant Necklace
+ Pea Coat
+ Knit Hat
+ Spring Print Scarf
+ Crossbody Bag
+ Metallic Flats

Outfit #75

Color Fitted Sweater
+ Neutral Skirt
+ Denim Vest
+ Leggings
+ Moccasins
+ Simple Stud Earrings
+ Neutral Scarf
+ Pea Coat
+ Knit Hat
+ Crossbody Bag
+ Riding Boots

OUTFITS 62-105: WINTER CASUAL

If your chambray dress is sleeveless, layer long-sleeve tee under or over dress. Then add quilted vest to finish off.

Outfit #76

Chambray Dress
+ Long Sleeve Navy Tee
+ Leggings
+ Quilted Vest
+ Wool Socks
+ Pearl Stud Earrings
+ Moto Jacket
+ Plaid Scarf
+ Knit Hat
+ Tote Bag
+ Riding Boots

Print tee over maxi dress. Add denim jacket to finish it off. When going out, swap denim jacket for pea coat for more warmth.

Outfit #76a

Black Maxi Dress
+ Print Tee #1
+ Denim Jacket
+ Cute Socks
+ Simple Stud Earrings
+ Pendant Necklace
+ Neutral Scarf
+ Gloves
+ Knit Hat
+ Crossbody Bag
+ Ankle Boots

OUTFITS 62-105: WINTER CASUAL

Outfit #77

Gray Tee
+ Dark Wash Jeans
+ Light Color Cardigan
+ Moccasins
+ Minimalist Necklace
+ Utility Jacket
+ Neutral Scarf
+ Gloves
+ Crossbody Tote
+ Riding Boots

Outfit #78

Graphic Tee
+ Dark Wash Jeans
+ Warm Pattern Cardigan
+ Cute Socks
+ Headband
+ Minimalist Bracelet
+ Pea Coat
+ Neutral Scarf
+ Tote Bag
+ Lace-Up Sneakers

OUTFITS 62-105: WINTER CASUAL

Shirt over dress.
Optional: Do an inside or outside gather on side- or center-front of shirt with coin + elastic. (Place coin on inside or outside of shirt; on opposite side, pull elastic over fabric and coin to create a gather.)

Outfit #79
Neutral Knee-Length Dress
+ Print Tee #1
+ Leggings
+ Denim Jacket
+ Wool Socks
+ Pearl Stud Earrings
+ Minimalist Bracelet
+ Pea Coat
+ Knit Hat
+ Neutral Scarf
+ Crossbody Bag
+ Riding Boots

Denim vest and belt added to break up the color. Belt in belt loops, with partial front tuck. (If color in pants and color in sweater don't work together, swap for a neutral top or bottom.)

Outfit #80a
Color Fitted Sweater
+ Color Pants
+ Denim Vest
+ Cute Socks
+ Neutral Belt
+ Pearl Stud Earrings
+ Fall/Winter Print Scarf
+ Pea Coat
+ Gloves
+ Tote Bag
+ Metallic Flats

OUTFITS 62-105: WINTER CASUAL

Outfit #80

White Fashion Tee
+ Dark Wash Jeans
+ Light Color Cardigan
+ Moccasins
+ Simple Stud Earrings
+ Sweatshirt/Hoodie
+ Knit Hat
+ Neutral Scarf
+ Crossbody Bag
+ Riding Boots

Swap cardigan with sweatshirt/hoodie when going out.

Outfit #81

Neutral Knee-Length Dress
+ Long Sleeve Navy Tee
+ Leggings
+ Wool Socks
+ Statement Earrings
+ Pendant Necklace
+ Moto Jacket
+ Knit Hat
+ Fall/Winter Print Scarf
+ Crossbody Bag
+ Riding Boots

Shirt over dress.
Optional: Do an inside or outside gather on side- or center-front of shirt with coin + elastic. (Place coin on inside or outside of shirt; on opposite side, pull elastic over fabric and coin to create a gather.)

OUTFITS 62-105: WINTER CASUAL

Add quilted vest or pea coat for additional warmth.

Outfit #82

Neutral Slouchy Sweater
+ Olive Pants
+ Moccasins
+ Minimalist Necklace
+ Pearl Stud Earrings
+ Plaid Scarf
+ Knit Hat
+ Tote Bag
+ Print Flats

Outfit #83

Slogan Tee
+ Slim Fit Athletic Pants
+ Warm Pattern Cardigan
+ Cute Socks
+ Headband
+ Utility Jacket
+ Knit Hat
+ Neutral Scarf
+ Crossbody Bag
+ Lace-Up Sneakers

OUTFITS 62-105: WINTER CASUAL

Sweater over chambray, with chambray sleeve cuffs either buttoned and poking out of sweater or unbuttoned and folded up over sweater.

Outfit #84

Chambray Button-Down
+ Olive Pants
+ Neutral Slouchy Sweater
+ Moccasins
+ Simple Stud Earrings
+ Moto Jacket
+ Gloves
+ Plaid Scarf
+ Crossbody Bag
+ Slip-On Sneakers

Outfit #85

White Fashion Tee
+ Slim Fit Athletic Pants
+ Light Color Cardigan
+ Moccasins
+ Statement Earrings
+ Pendant Necklace
+ Denim Jacket
+ Plaid Scarf
+ Knit Hat
+ Tote Bag
+ Lace-Up Sneakers

OUTFITS 62-105: WINTER CASUAL

Outfit #85a

Neutral Plaid Button-Down
+ Dark Wash Jeans
+ Color Fitted Sweater
+ Cute Socks
+ Pendant Necklace
+ Quilted Vest
+ Gloves
+ Spring Print Scarf
+ Crossbody Bag
+ Ankle Boots

Sweater over button-down. Fold button-down's cuffs up over sweater sleeves once or twice.
Roll pant hems 1-2" to wear with ankle boots.

Outfit #86

Print Sleeveless Top #1
+ Dark Wash Jeans
+ Dark Color Cardigan
+ Wool Socks
+ Statement Earrings
+ Color Belt
+ Pea Coat
+ Gloves
+ Fall/Winter Print Scarf
+ Tote Bag
+ Print Flats

Belt in belt loops. Optional partial front tuck.

OUTFITS 62-105: WINTER CASUAL

Outfit #87

Chambray Button-Down
+ Slim Fit Athletic Pants
+ Quilted Vest
+ Cute Socks
+ Simple Stud Earrings
+ Headband
+ Pea Coat
+ Neutral Scarf
+ Gloves
+ Crossbody Bag
+ Slip-On Sneakers

Optional partial front tuck.

Outfit #88

Color Plaid Button-Down
+ Neutral Jeans
+ Color Fitted Sweater
+ Moccasins
+ Pearl Stud Earrings
+ Utility Vest
+ Knit Hat
+ Neutral Scarf
+ Tote Bag
+ Riding Boots

Wear button-down under sweater with sleeves and collar poking out.

OUTFITS 62-105: WINTER CASUAL

Outfit #88a

Black Maxi Dress
+ Warm Pattern Cardigan
+ Moccasins
+ Pendant Necklace
+ Pea Coat
+ Gloves
+ Tote Bag
+ Riding Boots

Outfit #89

Neutral Knee-Length Dress
+ Warm Pattern Cardigan
+ Leggings
+ Wool Socks
+ Statement Earrings
+ Minimalist Necklace
+ Utility Jacket
+ Fall/Winter Print Scarf
+ Knit Hat
+ Crossbody Bag
+ Riding Boots

OUTFITS 62-105: WINTER CASUAL

Outfit #90

Long Sleeve Striped Tee
+ Dark Wash Jeans
+ Light Color Cardigan
+ Moccasins
+ Pearl Stud Earrings
+ Statement Bracelet
+ Pea Coat
+ Plaid Scarf
+ Gloves
+ Tote Bag
+ Metallic Flats

Outfit #90a

Neutral Slouchy Sweater
+ Dark Wash Jeans
+ Chambray Button-Down
+ Statement Earrings
+ Utility Jacket
+ Fall/Winter Print Scarf
+ Tote Bag
+ Riding Boots

Sweater over chambray, with chambray sleeve cuffs either buttoned and poking out of sweater or unbuttoned and folded up over sweater.

OUTFITS 62-105: WINTER CASUAL

Outfit #91

Color Tee
+ Dark Wash Jeans
+ Warm Pattern Cardigan
+ Wool Socks
+ Pearl Stud Earrings
+ Moto Jacket
+ Neutral Scarf
+ Gloves
+ Tote Bag
+ Riding Boots

Outfit #92

Neutral Tunic Sweater
+ Olive Pants
+ Cute Socks
+ Fall/Winter Print Scarf
+ Pearl Stud Earrings
+ Minimalist Bracelet
+ Moto Jacket
+ Gloves
+ Crossbody Bag
+ Ankle Boots

Optional partial tuck (if so, add belt at loops).
Roll pant hems 1-2" to wear with ankle boots.

OUTFITS 62-105: WINTER CASUAL

Optional partial tuck.

Outfit #93

Color Fitted Sweater
+ Slim Fit Athletic Pants
+ Moccasins
+ Minimalist Bracelet
+ Minimalist Necklace
+ Quilted Vest
+ Knit Hat
+ Plaid Scarf
+ Tote Bag
+ Lace-Up Sneakers

Outfit #94

Neutral Plaid Button-Down
+ Dark Wash Jeans
+ Dark Color Cardigan
+ Wool Socks
+ Statement Earrings
+ Headband
+ Pea Coat
+ Knit Hat
+ Neutral Scarf
+ Crossbody Bag
+ Lace-Up Sneakers

OUTFITS 62-105: WINTER CASUAL

Belt in belt loops. Partial tuck.
Roll pant hems 1-2" to wear with ankle boots.

Outfit #95

Print Tee #1
+ Dark Wash Jeans
+ Dark Color Cardigan
+ Moccasins
+ Simple Stud Earrings
+ Color Belt
+ Quilted Vest
+ Knit Hat
+ Plaid Scarf
+ Tote Bag
+ Ankle Boots

Outfit #95a

Neutral Tunic Sweater
+ Color Pants
+ Wool Socks
+ Headband
+ Utility Vest
+ Fall/Winter Print Scarf
+ Knit Hat
+ Crossbody Bag
+ Riding Boots

OUTFITS 62-105: WINTER CASUAL

Outfit #96

Neutral Slouchy Sweater
+ Neutral Jeans
+ Quilted Vest
+ Cute Socks
+ Pearl Stud Earrings
+ Utility Jacket
+ Fall/Winter Print Scarf
+ Gloves
+ Tote Bag
+ Ankle Boots

Roll pant hems 1-2" to wear with ankle boots.

Outfit #97

Long Sleeve Striped Tee
+ Slim Fit Athletic Pants
+ Cute Socks
+ Spring Print Scarf
+ Pearl Stud Earrings
+ Sweatshirt/Hoodie
+ Utility Vest
+ Knit Hat
+ Crossbody Bag
+ Slip-On Sneakers

Layer utility vest over sweatshirt/hoodie for warmth.

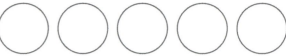

OUTFITS 62-105: WINTER CASUAL

Outfit #98

Neutral Slouchy Sweater
+ Neutral Skirt
+ Leggings
+ Cute Socks
+ Minimalist Necklace
+ Utility Jacket
+ Knit Hat
+ Gloves
+ Tote Bag
+ Riding Boots

Outfit #99

Neutral Tunic Sweater
+ Dark Wash Jeans
+ Cute Socks
+ Color Belt
+ Statement Earrings
+ Moto Jacket
+ Fall/Winter Print Scarf
+ Gloves
+ Tote Bag
+ Riding Boots

Belt over sweater below bust or at natural waist.

OUTFITS 62-105: WINTER CASUAL

Outfit #100

Neutral Tunic Top
+ Leggings
+ Warm Pattern Cardigan
+ Simple Stud Earrings
+ Minimalist Necklace
+ Pea Coat
+ Knit Hat
+ Gloves
+ Crossbody Bag
+ Riding Boots

Wear sweater over maxi dress.

Outfit #100a

Black Maxi Dress
+ Color Fitted Sweater
+ Moccasins
+ Plaid Scarf
+ Statement Earrings
+ Quilted Vest
+ Gloves
+ Tote Bag
+ Metallic Flats

OUTFITS 62-105: WINTER CASUAL

Outfit #101

Chambray Dress
+ Neutral Slouchy Sweater
+ Leggings
+ Wool Socks
+ Headband
+ Pendant Necklace
+ Utility Vest
+ Neutral Scarf
+ Gloves
+ Tote Bag
+ Riding Boots

Roll pant hems 1-2" to wear with ankle boots.

Outfit #102

Long Sleeve Navy Tee
+ Neutral Jeans
+ Quilted Vest
+ Moccasins
+ Simple Stud Earrings
+ Pendant Necklace
+ Pea Coat
+ Fall/Winter Print Scarf
+ Knit Hat
+ Crossbody Bag
+ Ankle Boots

OUTFITS 62-105: WINTER CASUAL

Outfit #103

Neutral Slouchy Sweater
+ Print Skirt
+ Leggings
+ Wool Socks
+ Statement Earrings
+ Utility Jacket
+ Neutral Scarf
+ Gloves
+ Tote Bag
+ Riding Boots

Belt in belt loops, partial tuck.

Outfit #104

Long Sleeve Navy Tee
+ Dark Wash Jeans
+ Light Color Cardigan
+ Cute Socks
+ Pendant Necklace
+ Neutral Belt
+ Pea Coat
+ Knit Hat
+ Spring Print Scarf
+ Crossbody Bag
+ Riding Boots

OUTFITS 62-105: WINTER CASUAL

Outfit #105

Neutral Slouchy Sweater
+ Slim Fit Athletic Pants
+ Utility Vest
+ Cute Socks
+ Pearl Stud Earrings
+ Pea Coat
+ Knit Hat
+ Neutral Scarf
+ Crossbody Bag
+ Slip-On Sneakers

Dressy Outfits for Winter
Outfits 106-115

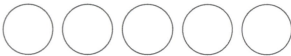

OUTFITS 106-115: WINTER DRESSY

Outfit #106

Striped Dress
+ Neutral Long Cardigan
+ Leggings
+ Statement Necklace
+ Simple Stud Earrings
+ Pea Coat
+ Fall/Winter Print Scarf
+ Tote Bag
+ Riding Boots

Outfit #107

Neutral Slouchy Sweater
+ Dark Wash Jeans
+ Spring Print Scarf
+ Statement Earrings
+ Pea Coat
+ Tote Bag
+ Ankle Boots

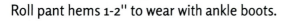

Roll pant hems 1-2" to wear with ankle boots.

OUTFITS 106-115: WINTER DRESSY

Outfit #108

Color Plaid Button-Down
+ Dark Wash Jeans
+ Neutral Slouchy Sweater
+ Neutral Belt
+ Statement Necklace
+ Moto Jacket
+ Tote Bag
+ Metallic Flats

Wear plaid top under sweater with sleeves folded or rolled over sweater. Statement necklace chain should lie under button-down collar with decorative design lying on sweater.

Outfit #109

Gray Tee
+ Print Skirt
+ Light Color Cardigan
+ Leggings
+ Pearl Stud Earrings
+ Statement Necklace
+ Moto Jacket
+ Neutral Scarf
+ Tote Bag
+ Riding Boots

OUTFITS 106-115: WINTER DRESSY

○ ○ ○ ○ ○

Outfit #110

Long Sleeve Striped Tee
+ Neutral Jeans
+ Moto Jacket
+ Statement Bracelet
+ Statement Earrings
+ Fall/Winter Print Scarf
+ Tote Bag
+ Color Flats

○ ○ ○ ○ ○

Outfit #111

Print Tee #1
+ Olive Pants
+ Neutral Long Cardigan
+ Statement Necklace
+ Pearl Stud Earrings
+ Pea Coat
+ Neutral Scarf
+ Tote Bag
+ Ankle Boots

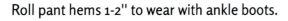

Roll pant hems 1-2" to wear with ankle boots.

OUTFITS 106-115: WINTER DRESSY

Belt in belt loops. Optional partial front tuck.

Outfit #112

Color Dressy Top
+ Dark Wash Jeans
+ Fall/Winter Print Scarf
+ Minimalist Bracelet
+ Statement Earrings
+ Pea Coat
+ Neutral Belt
+ Tote Bag
+ Metallic Flats

Roll pant hems 1-2" to wear with ankle boots.

Outfit #113

Color Dressy Top
+ Neutral Jeans
+ Plaid Scarf
+ Statement Bracelet
+ Simple Stud Earrings
+ Moto Jacket
+ Tote Bag
+ Ankle Boots

OUTFITS 106-115: WINTER DRESSY

Outfit #114

Neutral Tunic Sweater
+ Leggings
+ Plaid Scarf
+ Pendant Necklace
+ Pearl Stud Earrings
+ Pea Coat
+ Tote Bag
+ Riding Boots

Outfit #115

Color Fitted Sweater
+ Neutral Jeans
+ Minimalist Bracelet
+ Statement Necklace
+ Simple Stud Earrings
+ Moto Jacket
+ Tote Bag
+ Ankle Boots

Roll pant hems 1-2" to wear with ankle boots.

OUTFITS 106-115: WINTER DRESSY

Belt at natural waist or below bust
(whichever works more naturally for your dress's style).

Outfit #115a

Black Maxi Dress
+ Moto Jacket
+ Color Belt
+ Simple Stud Earrings
+ Minimalist Bracelet
+ Fall/Winter Print Scarf
+ Tote Bag
+ Metallic Flats

Casual Outfits for Spring
Outfits 116-168

OUTFITS 116-168: SPRING CASUAL

Outfit #116

Color Dressy Top
+ Light Wash Jeans
+ Spring Print Scarf
+ Pearl Stud Earrings
+ Neutral Belt
+ Neutral Long Cardigan
+ Tote Bag
+ Slip-On Sneakers

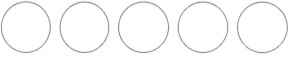

Outfit #116a

Chambray Button-Down
+ Color Pants
+ Pearl Stud Earrings
+ Minimalist Necklace
+ Utility Vest
+ Spring Print Scarf
+ Crossbody Bag
+ Print Flats

OUTFITS 116-168: SPRING CASUAL

Outfit #117

Print Sleeveless Top #2
+ Neutral Skirt
+ Light Color Cardigan
+ Statement Earrings
+ Crossbody Bag
+ Slide Sandals

Outfit #118

White Basic Tee
+ Neutral Skirt
+ Minimalist Necklace
+ Simple Stud Earrings
+ Denim Jacket
+ Spring Print Scarf
+ Tote Bag
+ Slide Sandals

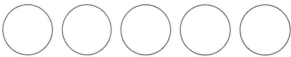

OUTFITS 116-168: SPRING CASUAL

Outfit #118a

Black Maxi Dress
+ Denim Jacket
+ Neutral Belt
+ Statement Necklace
+ Tote Bag
+ Print Flats

Belt at natural waist under denim jacket.

Outfit #119

Graphic Tee
+ Light Wash Jeans
+ Dark Color Cardigan
+ Pearl Stud Earrings
+ Headband
+ Spring Print Scarf
+ Crossbody Bag
+ Lace-Up Sneakers

OUTFITS 116-168: SPRING CASUAL

Outfit #120

White Fashion Tee
+ Print Skirt
+ Minimalist Bracelet
+ Statement Earrings
+ Utility Vest
+ Tote Bag
+ Color Flats

Outfit #120a

Short Sleeve Striped Tee
+ Color Pants
+ Neutral Belt
+ Minimalist Necklace
+ Pearl Stud Earrings
+ Utility Jacket
+ Spring Print Scarf
+ Tote Bag
+ Slip-On Sneakers

OUTFITS 116-168: SPRING CASUAL

Outfit #121

Print Tee #2
+ Neutral Skirt
+ Light Color Cardigan
+ Simple Stud Earrings
+ Tote Bag
+ Slide Sandals

Belt in belt loops, partial tuck.

Outfit #122

Color Sleeveless Top #2
+ Light Wash Jeans
+ Neutral Long Cardigan
+ Pendant Necklace
+ Neutral Belt
+ Tote Bag
+ Color Flats

OUTFITS 116-168: SPRING CASUAL

Outfit #123

Print Tee #2
+ Neutral Jeans
+ Neutral Long Cardigan
+ Pearl Stud Earrings
+ Pendant Necklace
+ Utility Jacket
+ Crossbody Bag
+ Slip-On Sneakers

Outfit #124

Print Knee-Length Dress
+ Neutral Fitted Tank
+ White Fashion Tee
+ Statement Earrings
+ Statement Bracelet
+ Denim Jacket
+ Nail Polish
+ Tote Bag
+ Fashion Sandals

Layering order: Dress, then tank, then white tee. (You are styling the dress as a skirt.) Tank used to avoid dress pattern showing through white tee. Paint toes for spring!

OUTFITS 116-168: SPRING CASUAL

Outfit #125

Color Sleeveless Top #1
+ Print Skirt
+ Neutral Long Cardigan
+ Pearl Stud Earrings
+ Pendant Necklace
+ Tote Bag
+ Color Flats

Outfit #126

Slogan Tee
+ Print Skirt
+ Denim Jacket
+ Statement Earrings
+ Crossbody Bag
+ Toe Nail Polish
+ Thong Sandals

119

OUTFITS 116-168: SPRING CASUAL

Outfit #126a

White Fashion Tee
+ Color Pants
+ Kimono
+ Pearl Stud Earrings
+ Minimalist Necklace
+ Tote Bag
+ Metallic Flats

Outfit #127

Color Sleeveless Top #2
+ Denim Shorts
+ Warm Pattern Cardigan
+ Simple Stud Earrings
+ Statement Necklace
+ Crossbody Bag
+ Slip-On Sneakers

OUTFITS 116-168: SPRING CASUAL

Outfit #128

Short Sleeve Striped Tee
+ Olive Pants
+ Denim Vest
+ Simple Stud Earrings
+ Minimalist Necklace
+ Spring Print Scarf
+ Crossbody Bag
+ Lace-Up Sneakers

Outfit #129

Print Dressy Top
+ Denim Shorts
+ Pendant Necklace
+ Neutral Scarf
+ Minimalist Bracelet
+ Moto Jacket
+ Tote Bag
+ Slip-On Sneakers

OUTFITS 116-168: SPRING CASUAL

Outfit #130

Color Sleeveless Top #2
+ Neutral Jeans
+ Kimono
+ Pearl Stud Earrings
+ Tote Bag
+ Slide Sandals

Outfit #131

Long Sleeve Striped Tee
+ Print Shorts
+ Neutral Long Cardigan
+ Color Belt
+ Simple Stud Earrings
+ Crossbody Bag
+ Metallic Flats

Whether this pattern mixing works will depend on the pattern of your shorts. You can also swap in any of the other shorts. Belt in belt loops with partial tuck.

OUTFITS 116-168: SPRING CASUAL

Outfit #132

Slogan Tee
+ Neutral Jeans
+ Light Color Cardigan
+ Minimalist Bracelet
+ Statement Necklace
+ Crossbody Bag
+ Fashion Sandals

Outfit #132a

Gray Tee
+ Color Pants
+ Sweatshirt/Hoodie
+ Pearl Stud Earrings
+ Baseball Cap
+ Crossbody Bag
+ Print Flats

Fold pant hems up once 3-4".

OUTFITS 116-168: SPRING CASUAL

Belt in belt loops, partial tuck.

Outfit #133

Color Sleeveless Top #1
+ Light Wash Jeans
+ Kimono
+ Neutral Belt
+ Simple Stud Earrings
+ Tote Bag
+ Slip-On Sneakers

Shirt over dress and vest over shirt. If your tee doesn't have a twist, tie a knot on side or front of shirt (can also do a gather by tying from inside).

Outfit #134

Print Knee-Length Dress
+ Color Tee
+ Feminine Vest
+ Pearl Stud Earrings
+ Denim Jacket
+ Tote Bag
+ Metallic Flats

OUTFITS 116-168: SPRING CASUAL

Outfit #135

Gray Tee
+ Light Wash Jeans
+ Utility Vest
+ Minimalist Bracelet
+ Simple Stud Earrings
+ Spring Print Scarf
+ Crossbody Bag
+ Lace-Up Sneakers

Outfit #135a

Black Maxi Dress
+ Graphic Tee
+ Headband
+ Denim Vest
+ Crossbody Bag
+ Slide Sandals

Wear shirt over dress. Tie a knot on side or front of shirt (can also do gather by tying from inside).

OUTFITS 116-168: SPRING CASUAL

Outfit #136

Print Tee #1
+ Color Shorts
+ Dark Color Cardigan
+ Statement Earrings
+ Tote Bag
+ Slip-On Sneakers

Outfit #137

Long Sleeve Striped Tee
+ Denim Shorts
+ Kimono
+ Pendant Necklace
+ Statement Bracelet
+ Tote Bag
+ Color Flats

Fold up shirt sleeves to elbow if a long sleeve shirt.

OUTFITS 116-168: SPRING CASUAL

Outfit #138

White Fashion Tee
+ Light Wash Jeans
+ Light Color Cardigan
+ Statement Necklace
+ Crossbody Bag
+ Fashion Sandals

Outfit #139

White Basic Tee
+ Print Skirt
+ Chambray Button-Down
+ Minimalist Bracelet
+ Statement Earrings
+ Moto Jacket
+ Crossbody Bag
+ Thong Sandals

Chambray over tee, either fully buttoned, middle buttoned with bottom ends tied or partially tucked.

OUTFITS 116-168: SPRING CASUAL

Outfit #139a

Print Tee #2
+ Color Pants
+ Feminine Vest
+ Minimalist Necklace
+ Utility Jacket
+ Tote Bag
+ Fashion Sandals

When going out, swap jacket with vest.

Outfit #140

Long Sleeve Striped Tee
+ Neutral Shorts
+ Denim Vest
+ Pendant Necklace
+ Simple Stud Earrings
+ Utility Jacket
+ Tote Bag
+ Slide Sandals

When going out, swap jacket with vest.

OUTFITS 116-168: SPRING CASUAL

Outfit #141

Chambray Button-Down
+ Neutral Shorts
+ Dark Color Cardigan
+ Neutral Belt
+ Pearl Stud Earrings
+ Spring Print Scarf
+ Tote Bag
+ Thong Sandals

Belt in belt loops, optional partial tuck.

Outfit #142

Gray Tee
+ Print Shorts
+ Utility Vest
+ Minimalist Necklace
+ Pearl Stud Earrings
+ Baseball Cap
+ Crossbody Bag
+ Slip-On Sneakers

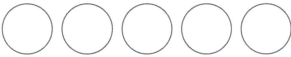

OUTFITS 116-168: SPRING CASUAL

Outfit #143

Color Sleeveless Top #1
+ Neutral Skirt
+ Spring Print Scarf
+ Statement Bracelet
+ Simple Stud Earrings
+ Tote Bag
+ Color Flats

Outfit #144

Short Sleeve Striped Tee
+ Dark Wash Jeans
+ Kimono
+ Minimalist Bracelet
+ Simple Stud Earrings
+ Tote Bag
+ Thong Sandals

OUTFITS 116-168: SPRING CASUAL

○ ○ ○ ○ ○

Wear shirt over dress. Tie a knot on side or front of shirt (can also do a gather by tying from inside).

Outfit #145

Neutral Knee-Length Dress
+ Graphic Tee
+ Minimalist Necklace
+ Simple Stud Earrings
+ Denim Jacket
+ Baseball Cap
+ Tote Bag
+ Slide Sandals

○ ○ ○ ○ ○

Outfit #146

Short Sleeve Striped Tee
+ Neutral Skirt
+ Light Color Cardigan
+ Simple Stud Earrings
+ Headband
+ Tote Bag
+ Metallic Flats

OUTFITS 116-168: SPRING CASUAL

Outfit #146a

Print Sleeveless Top #2
+ Color Pants
+ Denim Jacket
+ Pendant Necklace
+ Minimalist Bracelet
+ Crossbody Bag
+ Slide Sandals

Outfit #147

Color Tee
+ Neutral Skirt
+ Feminine Vest
+ Statement Earrings
+ Minimalist Bracelet
+ Spring Print Scarf
+ Tote Bag
+ Fashion Sandals

OUTFITS 116-168: SPRING CASUAL

Outfit #148

Chambray Button-Down
+ Neutral Jeans
+ Feminine Vest
+ Pearl Stud Earrings
+ Utility Jacket
+ Crossbody Bag
+ Print Flats

Optional: Fold up pant hems.

Outfit #149

Chambray Button-Down
+ Color Shorts
+ Neutral Belt
+ Minimalist Bracelet
+ Spring Print Scarf
+ Tote Bag
+ Slip-On Sneakers

Belt in belt loops, optional partial tuck.

OUTFITS 116-168: SPRING CASUAL

Outfit #150

Long Sleeve Striped Tee
+ Color Shorts
+ Denim Vest
+ Pendant Necklace
+ Simple Stud Earrings
+ Moto Jacket
+ Tote Bag
+ Lace-Up Sneakers

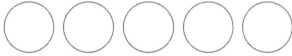

Outfit #150a

Color Tee
+ Olive Pants
+ Kimono
+ Simple Stud Earrings
+ Minimalist Necklace
+ Tote Bag
+ Fashion Sandals

OUTFITS 116-168: SPRING CASUAL

Optional: Fold up pant hems.

Outfit #151

Print Tee #1
+ Neutral Jeans
+ Light Color Cardigan
+ Statement Necklace
+ Minimalist Bracelet
+ Tote Bag
+ Slip-On Sneakers

Outfit #152

Slogan Tee
+ Neutral Skirt
+ Headband
+ Statement Earrings
+ Denim Jacket
+ Sunglasses
+ Crossbody Tote
+ Slide Sandals

OUTFITS 116-168: SPRING CASUAL

Outfit #152a

Black Maxi Dress
+ Denim Vest
+ Pendant Necklace
+ Pearl Stud Earrings
+ Spring Print Scarf
+ Crossbody Bag
+ Color Flats

Outfit #153

Color Sleeveless Top #1
+ Denim Shorts
+ Kimono
+ Pearl Stud Earrings
+ Minimalist Necklace
+ Crossbody Bag
+ Metallic Flats

OUTFITS 116-168: SPRING CASUAL

Outfit #154

Print Tee #1
+ Neutral Skirt
+ Utility Vest
+ Pearl Stud Earrings
+ Headband
+ Tote Bag
+ Thong Sandals

Optional: Fold up pant hems.

Outfit #155

Color Tee
+ Neutral Jeans
+ Denim Vest
+ Minimalist Bracelet
+ Simple Stud Earrings
+ Pendant Necklace
+ Spring Print Scarf
+ Tote Bag
+ Lace-Up Sneakers

OUTFITS 116-168: SPRING CASUAL

Outfit #156

Print Tee #2
+ Light Wash Jeans
+ Neutral Long Cardigan
+ Pearl Stud Earrings
+ Statement Necklace
+ Crossbody Bag
+ Slip-On Sneakers

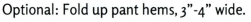

Optional: Fold up pant hems, 3"-4" wide.

Outfit #156a

Neutral Knee-Length Dress
+ Dark Color Cardigan
+ Simple Stud Earrings
+ Minimalist Necklace
+ Baseball Cap
+ Crossbody Bag
+ Print Flats

OUTFITS 116-168: SPRING CASUAL

Outfit #157

Color Sleeveless Top #2
+ Dark Wash Jeans
+ Neutral Long Cardigan
+ Statement Earrings
+ Minimalist Necklace
+ Tote Bag
+ Color Flats

Optional partial tuck.

Outfit #158

Print Sleeveless Top #2
+ Light Wash Jeans
+ Neutral Belt
+ Pearl Stud Earrings
+ Minimalist Necklace
+ Sweatshirt/Hoodie
+ Crossbody Bag
+ Fashion Sandals

Belt in belt loops with optional tuck.

OUTFITS 116-168: SPRING CASUAL

Outfit #159

Print Knee-Length Dress
+ Denim Vest
+ Statement Earrings
+ Pendant Necklace
+ Statement Bracelet
+ Tote Bag
+ Slide Sandals

Outfit #160

White Basic Tee
+ Light Wash Jeans
+ Light Color Cardigan
+ Simple Stud Earrings
+ Pendant Necklace
+ Spring Print Scarf
+ Crossbody Bag
+ Print Flats

OUTFITS 116-168: SPRING CASUAL

Belt in loops, partial tuck (to break up the color).

Outfit #160a

Graphic Tee
+ Color Pants
+ Denim Jacket
+ Neutral Belt
+ Pearl Stud Earrings
+ Tote Bag
+ Metallic Flats

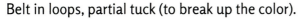

Outfit #161

Print Sleeveless Top #1
+ Neutral Skirt
+ Light Color Cardigan
+ Statement Earrings
+ Pendant Necklace
+ Tote Bag
+ Thong Sandals

OUTFITS 116-168: SPRING CASUAL

Outfit #162

Chambray Button-Down
+ Print Shorts
+ Neutral Fitted Tank
+ Color Belt
+ Simple Stud Earrings
+ Crossbody Bag
+ Slip-On Sneakers

Belt in loops with tank fully tucked into shorts. Layer chambray over tank, open with ends tied on the front.

Outfit #163

Color Tee
+ Light Wash Jeans
+ Warm Pattern Cardigan
+ Neutral Belt
+ Pearl Stud Earrings
+ Minimalist Necklace
+ Tote Bag
+ Color Flats

Belt in belt loops, partial tuck (leave untucked if tee has twist like the exact tee).

OUTFITS 116-168: SPRING CASUAL

Outfit #164

Color Tee
+ Print Skirt
+ Feminine Vest
+ Headband
+ Denim Jacket
+ Crossbody Bag
+ Thong Sandals

When going out, swap jacket with vest.

Outfit #165

White Basic Tee
+ Neutral Jeans
+ Denim Jacket
+ Neutral Belt
+ Statement Earrings
+ Pendant Necklace
+ Spring Print Scarf
+ Tote Bag
+ Color Flats

Belt in belt loops, partial front tuck (to break up the white).

OUTFITS 116-168: SPRING CASUAL

Outfit #165a

Striped Dress
+ Dark Color Cardigan
+ Simple Stud Earrings
+ Minimalist Necklace
+ Baseball Cap
+ Crossbody Bag
+ Lace-Up Sneakers

Outfit #166

Print Sleeveless Top #1
+ Neutral Jeans
+ Light Color Cardigan
+ Statement Earrings
+ Denim Jacket
+ Tote Bag
+ Slip-On Sneakers

When going out either add jacket or swap with cardigan.

OUTFITS 116-168: SPRING CASUAL

When going out either add jacket or swap with cardigan. Belt in belt loops, optional partial tuck.

Outfit #167

Slogan Tee
+ Light Wash Jeans
+ Light Color Cardigan
+ Neutral Belt
+ Pearl Stud Earrings
+ Utility Jacket
+ Crossbody Bag
+ Lace-Up Sneakers

Belt in belt loops, partial tuck or tie a knot as pictured.

Outfit #168

Graphic Tee
+ Neutral Jeans
+ Neutral Long Cardigan
+ Color Belt
+ Simple Stud Earrings
+ Crossbody Bag
+ Thong Sandals

Dressy Outfits for Spring
Outfits 169-178

OUTFITS 169-178: SPRING DRESSY

Outfit #169

Striped Dress
+ Kimono
+ Color Belt
+ Pearl Stud Earrings
+ Tote Bag
+ Color Flats

Belt at natural waist.

Outfit #170

Print Dressy Top
+ Neutral Shorts
+ Neutral Belt
+ Pendant Necklace
+ Statement Earrings
+ Denim Jacket
+ Tote Bag
+ Fashion Sandals

Belt in belt loops, optional partial tuck.

OUTFITS 169-178: SPRING DRESSY

Outfit #171a

Black Maxi Dress
+ Light Color Cardigan
+ Statement Necklace
+ Tote Bag
+ Thong Sandals

Outfit #171

Color Dressy Top
+ Print Skirt
+ Feminine Vest
+ Pearl Stud Earrings
+ Pendant Necklace
+ Tote Bag
+ Thong Sandals

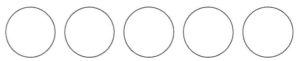

OUTFITS 169-178: SPRING DRESSY

Outfit #172

Neutral Dressy Top
+ Olive Pants
+ Neutral Belt
+ Minimalist Bracelet
+ Simple Stud Earrings
+ Minimalist Necklace
+ Denim Jacket
+ Tote Bag
+ Metallic Flats

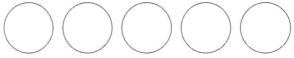

Outfit #173

Chambray Dress
+ Feminine Vest
+ Statement Earrings
+ Minimalist Bracelet
+ Tote Bag
+ Color Flats

OUTFITS 169-178: SPRING DRESSY

Outfit #174

Neutral Dressy Top
+ Neutral Jeans
+ Light Color Cardigan
+ Simple Stud Earrings
+ Pendant Necklace
+ Spring Print Scarf
+ Tote Bag
+ Color Flats

Outfit #175

Color Dressy Top
+ Neutral Skirt
+ Kimono
+ Statement Earrings
+ Minimalist Necklace
+ Tote Bag
+ Fashion Sandals

OUTFITS 169-178: SPRING DRESSY

○ ○ ○ ○ ○

Outfit #176

Neutral Dressy Top
+ Print Skirt
+ Denim Jacket
+ Pearl Stud Earrings
+ Statement Necklace
+ Tote Bag
+ Slide Sandals

○ ○ ○ ○ ○

Outfit #177a

Print Dressy Top
+ Color Pants
+ Feminine Vest
+ Statement Necklace
+ Simple Stud Earrings
+ Tote Bag
+ Metallic Flats

OUTFITS 169-178: SPRING DRESSY

Belt at waist (in place of sash if wearing the exact dress).

Outfit #177

Neutral Knee-Length Dress
+ Light Color Cardigan
+ Neutral Belt
+ Statement Bracelet
+ Statement Earrings
+ Pendant Necklace
+ Tote Bag
+ Thong Sandals

Outfit #178

Short Sleeve Striped Tee
+ Neutral Jeans
+ Statement Necklace
+ Statement Earrings
+ Kimono
+ Tote Bag
+ Color Flats

Casual Outfits for Summer
Outfits 179-229

OUTFITS 179-229: SUMMER CASUAL

Outfit #179

Color Sleeveless Top #1
+ Color Shorts
+ Pendant Necklace
+ Pearl Stud Earrings
+ Kimono
+ Sunglasses
+ Nail Polish
+ Crossbody Bag
+ Thong Sandals

Get a fresh coat of nail polish on the toes and pull out the sunglasses! When not in use, pop sunglasses on head for chic accessory.

Outfit #180

ray Tee
+ Neutral Skirt
+ Denim Vest
+ Statement Necklace
+ Crossbody Bag
+ Slip-On Sneakers

OUTFITS 179-229: SUMMER CASUAL

Outfit #181

White Fashion Tee
+ Color Shorts
+ Statement Necklace
+ Kimono
+ Crossbody Bag
+ Slip-On Sneakers

Outfit #182

Neutral Knee-Length Dress
+ Simple Stud Earrings
+ Statement Bracelet
+ Denim Vest
+ Crossbody Bag
+ Fashion Sandals

OUTFITS 179-229: SUMMER CASUAL

○ ○ ○ ○ ○

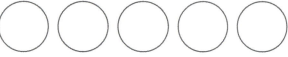

Outfit #183

Print Tee #1
+ Denim Shorts
+ Pearl Stud Earrings
+ Pendant Necklace
+ Neutral Belt
+ Tote Bag
+ Lace-up Sneakers

Belt in belt loops, partial tuck.

○ ○ ○ ○ ○

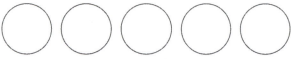

Outfit #183a

White Basic Tee
+ Color Pants
+ Headband
+ Minimalist Necklace
+ Crossbody Bag
+ Slide Sandals

OUTFITS 179-229: SUMMER CASUAL

○ ○ ○ ○ ○

Outfit #184

Gray Tee
+ Color Shorts
+ Pearl Stud Earrings
+ Denim Vest
+ Baseball Cap
+ Tote Bag
+ Color Flats

○ ○ ○ ○ ○

Outfit #185

Short Sleeve Striped Tee
+ Color Shorts
+ Kimono
+ Simple Stud Earrings
+ Minimalist Bracelet
+ Tote Bag
+ Fashion Sandals

OUTFITS 179-229: SUMMER CASUAL

○ ○ ○ ○ ○

Belt at cinching/natural waist. Works best on dresses without drawstrings.

Outfit #186

Chambray Dress
+ Neutral Belt
+ Pendant Necklace
+ Tote Bag
+ Thong Sandals

○ ○ ○ ○ ○

Outfit #187

Gray Tee
+ Denim Shorts
+ Kimono
+ Simple Stud Earrings
+ Pendant Necklace
+ Tote Bag
+ Fashion Sandals

OUTFITS 179-229: SUMMER CASUAL

○ ○ ○ ○ ○

Outfit #188

Belt in belt loops, partial tuck.

White Fashion Tee
+ Denim Shorts
+ Neutral Belt
+ Pendant Necklace
+ Crossbody Bag
+ Lace-Up Sneakers

○ ○ ○ ○ ○

Outfit #189

Graphic Tee
+ Neutral Shorts
+ Denim Vest
+ Minimalist Bracelet
+ Crossbody Bag
+ Slide Sandals

OUTFITS 179-229: SUMMER CASUAL

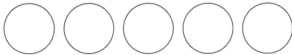

Outfit #190

Neutral Tunic Top
+ Denim Shorts
+ Feminine Vest
+ Statement Necklace
+ Crossbody Bag
+ Slip-On Sneakers

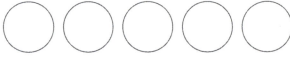

Layer gray tee over maxi dress.

Outfit #190a

Black Maxi Dress
+ Gray Tee
+ Pearl Stud Earrings
+ Headband
+ Crossbody Bag
+ Thong Sandals

OUTFITS 179-229: SUMMER CASUAL

Outfit #191

Short Sleeve Striped Tee
+ Denim Shorts
+ Neutral Belt
+ Statement Necklace
+ Pearl Stud Earrings
+ Baseball Cap
+ Tote Bag
+ Thong Sandals

Belt in belt loops, partial tuck.

Outfit #192

Slogan Tee
+ Print Shorts
+ Statement Bracelet
+ Pearl Stud Earrings
+ Baseball Cap
+ Crossbody Bag
+ Slide Sandals

Belt in belt loops, optional partial tuck.

OUTFITS 179-229: SUMMER CASUAL

○ ○ ○ ○ ○

Outfit #193

Print Sleeveless Top #1
+ Neutral Shorts
+ Statement Necklace
+ Simple Stud Earrings
+ Denim Vest
+ Sunglasses
+ Tote Bag
+ Thong Sandals

○ ○ ○ ○ ○

Outfit #194

Graphic Tee
+ Neutral Skirt
+ Pearl Stud Earrings
+ Baseball Cap
+ Tote Bag
+ Fashion Sandals

Untied, partial front tuck.

162

OUTFITS 179-229: SUMMER CASUAL

Outfit #195

Print Tee #2
+ Neutral Shorts
+ Statement Earrings
+ Minimalist Bracelet
+ Crossbody Bag
+ Color Flats

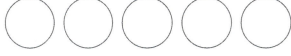

Outfit #195a

Print Tee #1
+ Color Pants
+ Minimalist Bracelet
+ Minimalist Necklace
+ Tote Bag
+ Fashion Sandals

OUTFITS 179-229: SUMMER CASUAL

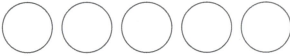

Outfit #196

Slogan Tee
+ Color Shorts
+ Neutral Belt
+ Minimalist Necklace
+ Pearl Stud Earrings
+ Tote Bag
+ Thong Sandals

Belt in belt loops, optional partial tuck.

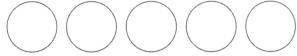

Outfit #197

White Fashion Tee
+ Neutral Skirt
+ Statement Bracelet
+ Minimalist Necklace
+ Simple Stud Earrings
+ Crossbody Bag
+ Slide Sandals

OUTFITS 179-229: SUMMER CASUAL

○ ○ ○ ○ ○

Outfit #198

White Basic Tee
+ Print Shorts
+ Color Belt
+ Minimalist Necklace
+ Baseball Cap
+ Tote Bag
+ Thong Sandals

Belt in belt loops.

○ ○ ○ ○ ○

Outfit #199

Print Tee #2
+ Color Shorts
+ Feminine Vest
+ Pearl Stud Earrings
+ Headband
+ Tote Bag
+ Slide Sandals

OUTFITS 179-229: SUMMER CASUAL

Belt in belt loops, optional partial tuck.

Outfit #200

Print Tee #2
+ Denim Shorts
+ Utility Vest
+ Simple Stud Earrings
+ Neutral Belt
+ Crossbody Bag
+ Thong Sandals

Belt in belt loops, partial tuck.

Outfit #201

Gray Tee
+ Neutral Shorts
+ Denim Vest
+ Color Belt
+ Pendant Necklace
+ Baseball Cap
+ Tote Bag
+ Thong Sandals

OUTFITS 179-229: SUMMER CASUAL

Outfit #201a

Black Maxi Dress
+ Neutral Belt
+ Simple Stud Earrings
+ Baseball Cap
+ Crossbody Bag
+ Slide Sandals

Outfit #202

Color Sleeveless Top #2
+ Print Skirt
+ Pendant Necklace
+ Pearl Stud Earrings
+ Tote Bag
+ Fashion Sandals

OUTFITS 179-229: SUMMER CASUAL

Outfit #203

Color Sleeveless Top #1
+ Neutral Jeans
+ Neutral Belt
+ Headband
+ Simple Stud Earrings
+ Tote Bag
+ Thong Sandals

Fold up pant hems 3-4". Belt in belt loops, partial tuck.

Outfit #203a

Color Sleeveless Top #1
+ Color Pants
+ Feminine Vest
+ Pearl Stud Earrings
+ Minimalist Bracelet
+ Crossbody Bag
+ Fashion Sandals

OUTFITS 179-229: SUMMER CASUAL

○ ○ ○ ○ ○

Outfit #204

Color Sleeveless Top #2
+ Neutral Skirt
+ Denim Vest
+ Pearl Stud Earrings
+ Pendant Necklace
+ Tote Bag
+ Thong Sandals

If wearing denim vest, try a full tuck. Pull up on front to loosen tuck.

○ ○ ○ ○ ○

Outfit #205

White Basic Tee
+ Denim Shorts
+ Feminine Vest
+ Pendant Necklace
+ Simple Stud Earrings
+ Crossbody Bag
+ Color Flats

OUTFITS 179-229: SUMMER CASUAL

Outfit #206

Graphic Tee
+ Denim Shorts
+ Statement Necklace
+ Crossbody Bag
+ Thong Sandals

Outfit #207

Color Dressy Top
+ Denim Shorts
+ Neutral Belt
+ Pendant Necklace
+ Pearl Stud Earrings
+ Tote Bag
+ Slip-On Sneakers

OUTFITS 179-229: SUMMER CASUAL

Outfit #208

Color Tee
+ Denim Shorts
+ Statement Bracelet
+ Pearl Stud Earrings
+ Crossbody Bag
+ Print Flats

Outfit #209

Color Tee
+ Neutral Shorts
+ Denim Vest
+ Neutral Belt
+ Statement Necklace
+ Tote Bag
+ Lace-Up Sneakers

Belt in belt loops, optional partial tuck.

OUTFITS 179-229: SUMMER CASUAL

Outfit #210

Short Sleeve Striped Tee
+ Neutral Shorts
+ Denim Vest
+ Minimalist Bracelet
+ Pendant Necklace
+ Tote Bag
+ Fashion Sandals

Fold pant hems up once, 3-4" wide.

Outfit #210a

Print Sleeveless Top #1
+ Color Pants
+ Pearl Stud Earrings
+ Baseball Cap
+ Crossbody Bag
+ Slide Sandals

OUTFITS 179-229: SUMMER CASUAL

○ ○ ○ ○ ○

Outfit #211

Color Tee
+ Print Shorts
+ Statement Bracelet
+ Pendant Necklace
+ Crossbody Bag
+ Slip-On Sneakers

○ ○ ○ ○ ○

Outfit #212

Print Sleeveless Top #2
+ Denim Shorts
+ Feminine Vest
+ Pendant Necklace
+ Pearl Stud Earrings
+ Crossbody Bag
+ Fashion Sandals

OUTFITS 179-229: SUMMER CASUAL

○ ○ ○ ○ ○

Belt in belt loops, partial tuck.

Outfit #213

Print Sleeveless Tee #2
+ Neutral Shorts
+ Statement Earrings
+ Color Belt
+ Tote Bag
+ Thong Sandals

○ ○ ○ ○ ○

Outfit #213a

Black Maxi Dress
+ Feminine Vest
+ Statement Necklace
+ Tote Bag
+ Slide Sandals

OUTFITS 179-229: SUMMER CASUAL

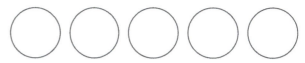

Outfit #214

Slogan Tee
+ Neutral Shorts
+ Denim Vest
+ Headband
+ Statement Earrings
+ Tote Bag
+ Slide Sandals

Outfit #214a

Neutral Fitted Tank
+ Color Pants
+ Kimono
+ Pearl Stud Earrings
+ Crossbody Bag
+ Slide Sandals

OUTFITS 179-229: SUMMER CASUAL

Outfit #215

Print Sleeveless Top #1
+ Denim Shorts
+ Feminine Vest
+ Pearl Stud Earrings
+ Pendant Necklace
+ Crossbody Bag
+ Color Flats

Optional: Add color belt on shorts.

Outfit #216

Neutral Tunic Top
+ Neutral Shorts
+ Pendant Necklace
+ Pearl Stud Earrings
+ Crossbody Bag
+ Thong Sandals

OUTFITS 179-229: SUMMER CASUAL

Outfit #217

Slogan Tee
+ Denim Shorts
+ Utility Vest
+ Simple Stud Earrings
+ Tote Bag
+ Fashion Sandals

Outfit #218

Print Tee #1
+ Neutral Shorts
+ Denim Vest
+ Statement Necklace
+ Simple Stud Earrings
+ Crossbody Bag
+ Lace-Up Sneakers

OUTFITS 179-229: SUMMER CASUAL

Outfit #219

White Basic Tee
+ Print Shorts
+ Statement Bracelet
+ Headband
+ Tote Bag
+ Color Flats

Outfit #220

Graphic Tee
+ Color Shorts
+ Denim Vest
+ Neutral Belt
+ Statement Earrings
+ Crossbody Bag
+ Slip-On Sneakers

Belt in belt loops.
Untie knot and do partial front tuck to break up color.

OUTFITS 179-229: SUMMER CASUAL

Outfit #220a

Slogan Tee
+ Color Pants
+ Statement Earrings
+ Baseball Cap
+ Crossbody Bag
+ Lace-Up Sneakers

Fold pant hems up once, 3-4" wide.

Outfit #221

Print Sleeveless Top #2
+ Color Shorts
+ Minimalist Necklace
+ Headband
+ Tote Bag
+ Print Flats

179

OUTFITS 179-229: SUMMER CASUAL

Outfit #222

Color Sleeveless Top #1
+ Print Shorts
+ Denim Vest
+ Simple Stud Earrings
+ Minimalist Bracelet
+ Crossbody Bag
+ Thong Sandals

Optional partial tuck.

Outfit #223

Color Sleeveless Top #2
+ Print Shorts
+ Feminine Vest
+ Statement Earrings
+ Tote Bag
+ Slide Sandals

OUTFITS 179-229: SUMMER CASUAL

Outfit #224

Neutral Dressy Top
+ Light Wash Jeans
+ Feminine Vest
+ Statement Bracelet
+ Pearl Stud Earrings
+ Tote Bag
+ Thong Sandals

Outfit #225

White Basic Tee
+ Print Skirt
+ Denim Vest
+ Pendant Necklace
+ Simple Stud Earrings
+ Crossbody Bag
+ Slide Sandals

OUTFITS 179-229: SUMMER CASUAL

Outfit #226

White Basic Tee
+ Color Shorts
+ Statement Necklace
+ Pearl Stud Earrings
+ Tote Bag
+ Fashion Sandals

Outfit #227

Color Sleeveless Top #1
+ Neutral Shorts
+ Color Belt
+ Statement Earrings
+ Baseball Cap
+ Crossbody Bag
+ Slip-On Sneakers

Belt in belt loops, partial tuck.

OUTFITS 179-229: SUMMER CASUAL

Outfit #228

Neutral Dressy Top
+ Denim Shorts
+ Color Belt
+ Minimalist Necklace
+ Crossbody Bag
+ Fashion Sandals

Belt in belt loops, optional partial tuck.

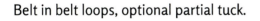

Outfit #228a

Neutral Fitted Tank
+ Dark Wash Jeans
+ Kimono
+ Minimalist Necklace
+ Crossbody Bag
+ Slide Sandals

OUTFITS 179-229: SUMMER CASUAL

Belt in belt loops, partial tuck.

Outfit #229

Color Sleeveless Top #2
+ Neutral Shorts
+ Neutral Belt
+ Statement Necklace
+ Crossbody Bag
+ Color Flats

Dressy Outfits for Summer
Outfits 230-239

OUTFITS 230-239: SUMMER DRESSY

Outfit #230

Print Dressy Top
+ Neutral Skirt
+ Feminine Vest
+ Pearl Stud Earrings
+ Pendant Necklace
+ Tote Bag
+ Metallic Flats

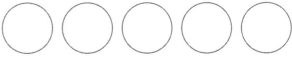

Outfit #231

Print Sleeveless Top #1
+ Color Shorts
+ Denim Vest
+ Color Belt
+ Statement Necklace
+ Minimalist Bracelet
+ Tote Bag
+ Color Flats

OUTFITS 230-239: SUMMER DRESSY

Outfit #232

Print Knee-Length Dress
+ Color Belt
+ Statement Necklace
+ Pearl Stud Earrings
+ Feminine Vest
+ Tote Bag
+ Color Flats

Outfit #233

Neutral Dressy Top
+ Neutral Shorts
+ Color Belt
+ Minimalist Necklace
+ Statement Earrings
+ Denim Vest
+ Tote Bag
+ Print Flats

Belt in belt loops, partial tuck.

OUTFITS 230-239: SUMMER DRESSY

Outfit #233a

Neutral Dressy Top
+ Color Pants
+ Kimono
+ Simple Stud Earrings
+ Pendant Necklace
+ Tote Bag
+ Fashion Sandals

Outfit #234

Neutral Knee-Length Dress
+ Feminine Vest
+ Simple Stud Earrings
+ Pendant Necklace
+ Tote Bag
+ Print Flats

OUTFITS 230-239: SUMMER DRESSY

Outfit #235

Color Dressy Top
+ Print Shorts
+ Minimalist Bracelet
+ Statement Earrings
+ Tote Bag
+ Metallic Flats

Outfit #236

Neutral Dressy Top
+ Color Shorts
+ Denim Vest
+ Statement Necklace
+ Pearl Stud Earrings
+ Tote Bag
+ Thong Sandals

OUTFITS 230-239: SUMMER DRESSY

Outfit #237

Color Dressy Top
+ Neutral Shorts
+ Feminine Vest
+ Minimalist Bracelet
+ Pearl Stud Earrings
+ Tote Bag
+ Metallic Flats

Outfit #238

Neutral Dressy Top
+ Print Shorts
+ Feminine Vest
+ Pendant Necklace
+ Crossbody Bag
+ Fashion Sandals

OUTFITS 230-239: SUMMER DRESSY

Outfit #239

Neutral Dressy Top
+ Neutral Skirt
+ Statement Necklace
+ Statement Bracelet
+ Pearl Stud Earrings
+ Tote Bag
+ Color Flats

Part 4

The Appendix

Bonus Resources Included With Outfit Guide

Your Outfit Guide Suite includes all the following resources.
To access them all, use the dashboard access link on the next page.

Outfit Gallery Web App

Shopping Guide

Additional Pre-Designed Color Palettes

Mini Course on Applying & Customizing Your Capsule Plan

The eBook Download

Print Order Form

Print copy available for purchase

Copyright © 2016-2019 Frumpy Fighters LLC   WWW.NOWTHATICANDO.COM

Dashboard Access

To access all the resources in your outfit guide suite, go to your dashboard:
www.nowthaticando.com/yrw-dashboard

If this is your first time accessing the dashboard, create an account or sign in with an existing account. You would have an existing account if you've taken any courses by Frump Fighters.

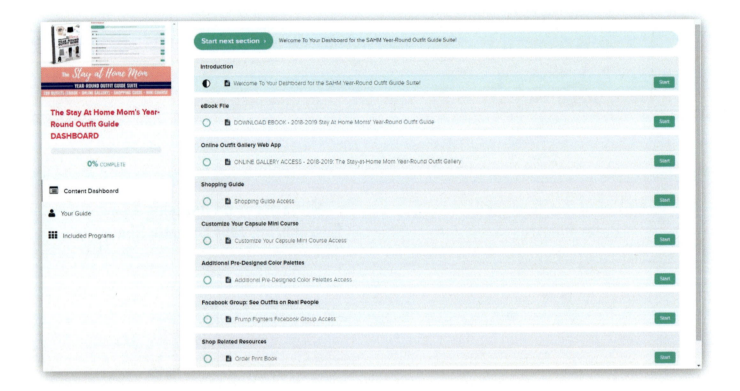

Shop Related Resources

Outfit Guides for Moms
Year-round, single season, and kids' guides.
www.nowthaticando.com/outfit-guides-checkout

Wardrobe Course: Frumpy to Fabulous
The custom approach to revamping your mom wardrobe.
www.nowthaticando.com/frumpy-to-fabulous

The Blog is Buzzing!
Visit the blog for ongoing tips on fighting the frump.
www.nowthaticando.com

Made in the USA
Lexington, KY
27 July 2019